KNACK™

BARTENDING BASICS

More than 400 Classic and Contemporary Cocktails for Any Occasion

CHERYL CHARMING

PHOTOGRAPHS BY Susan Bourgoin

KNACK™
MAKE IT EASY

Guilford, Connecticut
An imprint of The Globe Pequot Press

Editor-in-Chief: Maureen Graney
Editor: Katie Benoit
Cover Design: Paul Beatrice, Bret Kerr
Text Design: Paul Beatrice
Layout: Kevin Mak
Cover photos by Susan Bourgoin
Interior photos by Susan Bourgoin

Library of Congress Cataloging-in-Publication Data is available on file.

ISBN 978-1-59921-504-4

Acknowledgments

A round of toasts to Maureen Graney and Katie Benoit at GPP's Knack Books imprint with any cocktail in this book they choose. And "thank you" to June Clark at FinePrint Literary Management in New York City for all her hard work again.

A big "Tuaca the Dog" toast to Susan Bourgoin and Susan Lindsey at Visual Cuisines in Orlando, Florida. Thank you so much for the stunning photography.

A Champagne cocktail tower of toasts to all my cocktail culture friends and acquaintances who have supported me over the years. I'm proud to share part of this subculture of a culture with you during the second golden age of cocktails.

And, of course, thanks to my friends and family for their continued support. Especially to my mother, Babs.

Prop Credits

Bar tools and products provided by www.barproducts .com.

Cocktail sticks, picks, straws, and drink decoration novelties provided by Spirit Foodservice, Inc. (www.spiritfood service.com).

Photographer Acknowledgments

Many thanks to Maureen and Katie for trusting us with this project. And thanks to Cheryl Charming for making every day and every drink fun! Thank you to Maria Carpio for lending us her beautiful hands, and a big thank you to Lindsey for organizing everything for us with a smile on her face. Last but not least, thank you to God, who shows us His love for us by giving us such a fun job!

~Susan Bourgoin, Visual Cuisines, Inc.

CONTENTS

INTRODUCTION
Behind the Wood

Behind the wood: the shiny, jeweled bottles filled with potable potions, the liquid gold that flows from a tap, the thirst-quenching libations served in ice-frosted glassware, the intriguing tools and techniques, the enticing smells, sights, and sounds, the warm smile housed in a well-groomed body.

For centuries, being the body behind the wooden barrier (eventually abbreviated to "bar") has held a fascination for many. The flexible beauty of bartending is that its skills can be showcased on a small-scale, novice level at a home party, where just a few recipes can dazzle friends, or on a large, professional level that calls for an in-depth knowledge of mixology at a local establishment. So, there's a level for all, including you.

In 1976, I dipped my first toe into the hospitality biz water by landing a job as a pizza waitress at Ken's Pizza in Benton, Arkansas. Soon I left the small town of Benton and ,jumped in the big pond feet first as a server at my favorite theme restaurant in Little Rock, John Barleycorn's Vision. One night, the manager said that he needed a cocktail waitress for the upstairs bar and that I was to report to the bartender. My feelings were ambivalent; I was scared of the dimly lit room with tinkling glassware and echoes of laughter but extremely curious at the same time. After a couple of weeks working the bar, I applied as a cocktail waitress at a new nightclub called Cabaret, but my goal was to make it behind the copper-topped bar. I morphed into a bar sponge and sopped up everything bar related: recipes, trivia, bar tricks, techniques, and so on, and I was quickly promoted to bartender and then to head bartender.

Learning to make new drinks was fun to me (and is probably one of the reasons why you purchased or were given this book), but my fascination was to twist recipes, flavors, and presentations. I quickly realized that I was a small-town girl with big-city talent. I took a bartender position on a cruise ship in the Caribbean, traveled the

country, and then made my way to tending bar at Walt Disney World. Never the while did I stop scribbling on cocktail napkins all things bar- and cocktail-related that I came across. The end product is this, the book that you hold in your hands right now—thirty-three years of what I've learned as a bartender condensed into these pages, and I'm very grateful and honored to pass it on to you.

To develop the knack of how to tend bar—and the knack of how to make cocktails (because they are two different knacks)—it's always best to start with simple classic recipes so that you create a firm foundation of cock-

tail knowledge to build a skyscraper of cocktails upon. Almost every chapter in this book shows you the basics, and, with each baby-step turn of the page, you'll begin to see how a simple cocktail combined with imagination can be twisted into unlimited possibilities as long as you develop a knack for what flavors mix well together.

An important part of building a firm cocktail foundation is learning the history of a spirit, ingredient, or recipe used. I did not make this history connection until about twenty years into my bartending career. As an author, I was forced to look back and connect the cocktail culture dots of what I had experienced. It was then that it hit me as to why specific cocktails were developed, why cocktails had certain names, and why some recipes worked and others did not. As you flip through this book and read the tidbits of trivia and history, you'll discover that a cocktail time travel trail will start to link in your mind. For example, why aren't there any recipes from cocktail books of the mid-1800s that call for Coca-Cola? Answer: because Coca-Cola wasn't available until the 1890s. Why was the number one cocktail across America rum and Coke in 1945? Answer: a popular singing trio, the Andrew Sisters, came out with a hit calypso song entitled "Rum and Coca-Cola." This is a perfect historical example of

how the introduction of products and the influence of the media shape the cocktail culture timeline.

According to cocktail historian and author David Wondrich, the word *cocktail* first appeared in print in the *The Farmer's Cabinet* newspaper on April 28, 1803. An excerpt from the paper, in reference to the cocktail as a morning drink, reads: "Drank a glass of cocktail—excellent for the head . . . Call'd at the Doct's. [F]ound Burnham—he looked very wise—drank another glass of cocktail." Over the past two hundred plus years the artform of the cocktail has risen and fallen, but recently there has been a rebirth of the cocktail. Modern mixologists and liquid chefs are behind the wood, studying and respecting the historic cocktail, then twisting it with modern ingredients. A liquid culinary marriage using fresh ingredients is taking place, and it's catching on thanks to those souls dedicated to spreading the cocktail gospel. Even extinct and banned ingredients from cocktail books of the 1800s are being raised from the dead.

There are several types of bars and several types of bartenders behind the wood. The one you choose to be is up to you. Today, the bartender pendulum tends to swing from extreme-flair, bottle-flipping bartenders to the purist of the pure mixologists. More than likely you, like me, will fall somewhere between these two, but understand that something can be gained from both these extremes. Take what interests you and make it your own.

So let's recap: The first step in learning to bartend is to start crafting the classics. Next, study some cocktail history. After that, your hands will be itching to get some hands-on experience. To begin, pick out a few cocktails from this book that you'd like to make. For example, if you like margaritas, then turn to the margarita chapter and begin with the first three. Look in the directions for the ingredients needed to make these cocktails. Of course, you'll need to buy the booze, but there are other garnishes, mixers, tools, and gadgets involved, as well. There is a great bar tool source in Chapter 20 (Resources: Cream of the Crop), if you need it. But to begin, simply start with baby steps.

Practice your bartender mechanics by combining your bar tools with some bottles filled with water. Stand behind the wood (or ironing board) in your home and practice your pouring techniques. Practice shaking, stirring, measuring, muddling, layering, and more. As you develop these skills, strive for safety, cleanliness, and precision. These skills will come with repetition and a passion for being a good bartender. Learn to make one cocktail really well, and then move on to a new one. You'll soon get the knack of making a good drink. Next, you need to incorporate the knack of tending bar. Yes, this includes making cocktails but that is only a piece of the cocktail pie. Tending bar also includes personality, good groom-ing, a great smile, good memory, average math skills (if money is involved), efficiency, alcohol knowledge, and physical strength to carry heavy bottles of liquor and beer and to haul out the trash.

So, have you decided what kind of bartender you want to be behind the wood? Maybe you're interested in just having friends over to try a new concoction, and that's great! Maybe you want to make a living from it. Fantastic! Whatever your interest may be, my only hope is that the information from my experiences and the rich images in this book jumpstart your desire. Also, please visit my Web site at www.misscharming.com for more information. My best to you. Cheers!

POURERS & OPENERS

Learn basic tools and techniques all bartenders should know

One of the best tools you can invest in is a bottle pourer. Twisting off spirit bottle lids and "glug-glugging" spirits work well for a neat drink (*neat* means a drink poured straight from the bottle into a glass without ice), but for precise and smooth control, a pourer is the best choice. Simply screw off a bottle lid and then push the pourer into the bottle. If your bottle has a wide mouth, then you'll have to buy a wide pourer. If you're using pourers for a party, just keep your bottle lids un-til you are finished, then screw the lids back on. After you are comfortable with pouring, bump it up a notch and try a long pour. Simply raise the bottle higher, creating a longer stream of spirit. Then you can graduate to reverse pouring, which is grabbing the neck of the bottle in reverse and pouring.

Using exact measures in a cocktail is crucial, and that's why jiggers and measuring devices are helpful. There are many sizes to choose from, especially from the two-ended jiggers. I

Pourers and Pouring

- Pourers add a professional touch when making cocktails. Use them in bottles that are used most often.

- Pourers come with options such as color, size, and material (plastic or metal).

- When pouring, flip up the bottle quickly and vertically. Practice with a bottle of water.

- Cut (downward movement when finished pouring) quickly downward in a smooth motion.

Jiggers and Measures

- The most professional bartenders use jiggers and measuring glasses for accuracy.

- Invest in a couple of jiggers of different sizes.

- For control, rest the edge of the jigger on or near the lip of the glass so that it creates one fluid movement of pouring and dumping.

- Try to rinse out jiggers as you go, especially when using creamy liqueurs.

prefer the jiggers and measuring glasses that show the measured lines. These have a wider range of use.

Openers are tools that can open beer bottles, wine bottles, and cans. The cool, flat, hip beer bottle openers are called "speed openers," and they are designed for the speed needed behind a high-volume bar. They also come with many ways to store on your body, from magnet clips to retractable reels. For a medium- to low-volume use, my favorite is a chrome bottle opener ring because you can pop off the cap and aim for the trash can all in one motion. There are many amateur wine bottle openers on the market, from the rabbit to winged corkscrews, but you need to learn to use the waiter's corkscrew.

Openers

- Beer bottle opener types are plentiful and are available in hip, practical, and novelty.

- Buy the beer bottle opener that works best for your needs.

- Professionals will use nothing less than a waiter's wine tool to open wine bottles.

- Can openers punch open a can. They usually have a bottle opener on the other end as well.

Mixer Pourers

Depending on your situation and needs, transferring juice and mixers into plastic containers can be time saving, helpful, and more attractive. They come with a necked lid with a pour spout on the end. You can also soak off bottle labels and use bottles as mixer containers. Simply buy wide-spout pourers for them.

SHAKERS & STRAINERS
Learn techniques that will have you stirring and shaking

Mixing glasses can be used for stirring a cocktail, muddling, and for the other half of a Boston shaker.

Bar spoons have long, spiraled handles. They can be found with a variety of ends, such as the traditional red knob, disc, and even forked. The forked end is used to get olives from a jar. I find that using the disc-ended spoon works best when it comes to stirring.

The julep strainer is used with mixing glasses so that you can strain the cocktail without the ice falling into the glass. It fits concave into the glass.

There are two types of shakers: Boston and cobbler. The cobbler is the three-piece shaker that you shake and take off the little lid, then strain through the built-in strainer. These shakers became popular during Prohibition. They were produced in many novelty shapes, such as a boot, bullet, or lighthouse. *Stephen Visakay* owns the largest collection of shakers in ex-

Mixing Glass and Bar Spoon

- A mixing glass is a tempered 16-ounce glass. A thick, untempered pint glass can be substituted.

- Use a mixing glass when a recipe calls for stirring instead of shaking.

- Stirring chills a cocktail without adding air bubbles into the drink, as shaking does.

- Bar spoons are long so they can reach the top of tall glasses.

Julep Strainer

- The julep strainer is believed to have started as a tea strainer and crossed over to the bar in the late 1800s.

- The top two drinks that use a julep strainer are the Classic Martini and the Manhattan.

- Practice with a glass of ice water to develop the feel for this strainer.

- Vintage julep strainers can be found on online auctions.

istence (over 1000). He displays them in his book, *Vintage Bar Ware*. Jimbo Walker owns the world's second largest collection at almost 600 shakers.

The Boston is the shaker that serious and professional bartenders use. It consists of a mixing glass and a shaker tin. Just firmly tap on top of the glass to ensure a tight fit, then shake glass side up, not in front of you or by your side, but professionally over your shoulder, for a minimum of ten seconds. To release, hold vertically tin side down, then firmly tap on the top of the tin on the side of the glass that is not touching. Ice

is an important factor when making a cocktail. Ideal cocktail ice should be large. Preferably use a 1-inch ice cube. Large ice creates less water dilution and keeps cocktails cold longer.

Boston Shaker

- A basic Boston shaker consists of a 16-ounce mixing glass fitted inside a 28-ounce shaker tin.

- New sizes of shaker tins are available, from small (cheater tins) to large (mako tins) to accommodate all needs.

- Powder- and rubber-coated tins are available in a rainbow of colors, such as hot pink, neon green, black sparkle, white, and tie dye.

Hawthorne Strainer

- The Hawthorne strainer has a coiled ring that fits inside a shaker tin.

- This strainer requires a firm but light touch.

- When straining, press firmly inward toward the inside of the tin, not down, or else it

- will stop the flow of liquid and liquid will seep out the sides.

- Hawthorne strainers can be found in a variety of colors, styles, and coatings.

MUDDLING & LAYERING

Muddle and layer your way up to the next level of bartender techniques

Every bartender should know a few ways to strain a drink. You should now understand that straining is all about keeping ice and other large ingredients out of the cocktail. If you don't happen to have a julep or Hawthorne strainer, then you can split strain. This means that you are slightly splitting the mixing glass and shaker tin apart, creating a small opening

for the liquid to stream from. Another way to strain is to insert the clean bottom end of a mixing glass into the tin to hold back the ice. Double or fine straining is when you strain with one hand while the other holds a mesh strainer over the drink to catch herb particles, pulp, seeds, and so forth.

A muddler in its basic form is like a mortar and pestle that

Split Strain

Look for modern tins with built-in strain holes at the top.

- Begin by positioning yourself with feet slightly apart for proper grounding.

- Split straining takes a little practice, so start with a Boston shaker of ice and water until you master this technique.

- It helps to use a vinyl- or rubber-coated shaker tin so your hands can handle the cold.

- Bar supply stores sell modern tins with built-in strainers.

Muddling

- Never use a muddler that has been stained and varnished. This poison will flake off into a drink.

- The flat end is the business end of a muddler.

- Invest in a taller-than-normal muddler in case you find yourself muddling in a shaker tin.

- The most popular drink that requires a muddler is the Mojito.

mashes and grinds ingredients. A muddler is a long stick used to mash ingredients for drinks. This mashing releases the oils and flavors from ingredients. There is a variety of muddlers on the market, from vintage to modern.

Remember that practice makes perfect for this skill.

Layering

- Practice layering at home with ingredients from your kitchen such as oils, vinegars, water, and juice.

- Layering requires a steady hand.

- You can break the fall of the liquid with practically anything. Most bars use a spoon or cherry.

- When layering several spirits and liqueurs or several drinks, have all your bottles set in a row and ready to go.

Stylized Layering

Layering takes a bit of practice, but after you get it you got it. An advanced and stylized way to layer is to use a disc-ended bar spoon. The disc end goes into the glass, and you pour the spirit or liqueur on the spiral handle. It travels and spirals down into the glass.

5

SPECIAL TOUCHES
Chill out, then warm up to the idea of some special touch techniques

There's nothing worse than preparing a nicely chilled cocktail, then pouring it into a warm, room-temperature glass. The temperature of your cocktail immediately begins to rise. Always chill the glass before pouring a strained drink. Also, with the martini craze glasses have become very important. Look for smaller cocktail glasses that are no larger than 7

ounces to keep your cocktail chilly to the bitter end.

Making a hot drink in a room-temperature glass works the opposite way. Instantly the glass lowers the temperature. To avoid this, start with a preheated glass. Also some people like to have their cognac or brandy warmed. One way to accomplish this is to pour 2 ounces of hot water (like the hot water

Chill and Warm a Glass

- To chill, fill a glass with ice and water (or carbonated water) and allow to sit while you make the drink.

- Prechill glasses that will be used for cold strained cocktails.

- Another way to chill is to keep glasses in the freezer.

- To preheat a glass or mug, simply fill it with hot water, then allow it to sit for about thirty seconds.

Rim a Glass

- Rimming something on the rim of a glass requires two things: something wet or sticky and your chosen edible ingredient.

- Saucers and plates work well for holding your ingredients.

- Lemon juice mixes well with sugar-based rims, and lime juice mixes well with salted rims.

- Rimming ideas are limited only by your imagination.

from a coffee machine) into a brandy snifter and allow the glass to warm for about a minute. Pour the water out, then add the brandy. Take it another step and serve it with the snifter bowl rested in a glass filled with a little hot water so the steam warms the brandy.

Rimmers with ingredient compartments can be purchased at bar supply stores.

Colored and Flavored Rims

- Use plastic bags and food coloring to color salts and sugars.

- Visit cake and cookie decorating supply stores for a larger assortment of colorings and other edible items.

- Crush cookies and candy in plastic bags.

Sticking Power

The easiest way to wet the rim of a glass is to take a slice of citrus and rub it around the rim. But sometimes this is not enough sticking power to hold cookie and candy crumbs. You may have to use simple syrup, honey, or even Karo syrup. If you have the time, apply it with a paintbrush.

GARNISHES
Cut, zest, and flame your way down the cocktail-making technique trail

You must always take precautions when cutting fruit and garnishes. You may even consider wearing rubber gloves to avoid the sting of citrus fruit to your hands, and there are cut-proof gloves you can wear under the rubber gloves if desired. Always use a knife that is longer than the length or width of what you are cutting. Make sure you wash, rinse, and dry the

fruit and vegetables and don't forget to wash your hands. If your citrus is not organic, then don't scrub the skin because doing so will take off some of the wax that is sprayed on the citrus and doesn't make the fruit appear very appetizing. If your ingredients are organic, you won't have to scrub them as much. You can wash them in a solution of 3 cups water,

Cutting

- Always use a sharp knife when cutting and always pay close attention to what you are doing at all times.

- You can use serrated or regular knives to cut fruit. It's your preference.

- For fruits, don't use cutting boards that were previously used for cutting animal products or concentrated flavors like garlic.

- Place a wet towel under the cutting board for traction.

Zesting

- 1. When making a zest spiral, first cut off one end of the lemon, then hold both the fruit and the zester firmly in your hands.

- 2. Press and pull the zester around the fruit to cut off a spiral.

- With practice you'll be able to zest the entire lemon continuously.

- Use the multiholed part of the zester to make tiny, scraped zests.

3 cups white vinegar, and a heaping tablespoon of baking soda, then rinse and dry.

There are three types of zests. Each looks different and serves a different purpose. The long, spiraled zest that is made with a zester (also called channel knife) is twisted to release the oils, then rubbed on a glass rim or twisted over the top of the cocktail. Tiny, scraped zests are used for infusing spirits, making liqueurs, adding extra flavor to a shaken-then-strained cocktail, or mixing with ingredients for rimming. These two types of zesters can be found in an all-in-one tool, or they can

be purchased separately. In a pinch you can use a vegetable peeler as a makeshift zester, but it's better to just pay the $6 to own one. The third zest is a 1-inch oval slice from the rind of a navel orange or thick-skinned lemon. You use it to flame the oil for a cocktail, so when you hear the bar term *flamed zest*, this is what it means.

Flaming a Zest

- 1. To flame a zest, hold the oval shaped citrus zest about an inch from the top of the cocktail.

- 2. Then hold a flame above the edge of the glass.

- 3. In one motion, squeeze the zest so that the spray of citrus oil ignites the flame.

- 4. The burnt oil freefalls into the cocktail, creating a caramelized layer gently floating on top.

Butane and Sulfur

There is much controversy about using lighters and matches when flaming. If the butane from a lighter or the sulfur from a match bothers you (by making its way into the cocktail), then keep a covered, unscented candle and a little batch of bamboo sticks or toothpicks nearby to use.

BARTENDING TOOLS

Try your hand at some heavy-duty techniques to really juice things up

Blenders can range in price from $20 to $2,000. One that will last on your home counter for fifty years should have at least 2 horsepower and cost around $300. When blending, add your liquid ingredients first, then slowly add ice.

Manual juice extractors are available, but if you're serious about buying one, then you'll want one that's electric. It can extract the juice from dense ingredients such as carrots, rhubarb, ginger, wheatgrass, pineapple meat, pears, and apples. It will cost around $300 as well. Electric citrus juicers are used for citrus like oranges, grapefruit, and limes because you can't juice the peels through the extractor. Well, you can, but you don't want to because of their bitterness. You can juice citrus

Blending

- Cracked or small ice works best when making drinks in a blender.

- Start with less ice than you think you need because you can always add more.

- Strive for a pourable consistency, but if you go a notch over the thickness, simply use a bar spoon to help the mixture into the glass.

- You can use a blender to puree as well.

Electric Juicing

- Juice extractors are used for all vegetables and fruits except citrus.

- Juice only what you need for twelve hours because it will begin to spoil after that unless you freeze it.

- Electric citrus juicers are good for high-volume use.

- Valencia oranges are for juicing, and navel oranges are for garnishes.

meat through an extractor, but it foams. Besides, electric citrus juicers are economical. One for home use can be found in local stores for about $30.

Manual citrus juicers come with a variety of options. The most modern and popular to use for cocktails is the two-handled squeezer so that juice can be squeezed straight into the drink, mixing glass, or shaker tin.

Ice crushers are available in electric and manual forms as well. The one to choose is the one that best fits your needs.

Manual Juicing

- Manual juicers are good for low-volume use.

- Using room-temperature fruits will yield more juice.

- To avoid pulp and seeds, double-strain through a mesh strainer. An easy mesh strainer to use is a loose teacup steeper. It will sit perfectly in the glass as you squeeze into it.

- Store lemon and lime juice in condiment squeeze bottles for easy use.

Crushing Ice

- *Crushed ice* in bar terms doesn't necessarily mean ice crushed to snow consistency. However, you can use this form of ice if you find a recipe described as a frappe or mist. And also for a mint julep.

- Cracked ice can be made by placing ice cubes into a canvas bag, then hitting it with a large heavy object such as a muddler or rolling pin.

THE SMALLEST GLASSWARE
Learn the small differences between these pocket-sized glasses used behind the bar

Shot glasses come in a plethora of styles and can be made of almost anything. Some people even have a collection of shot glasses because wherever you travel you find these glasses in souvenir shops. Novelty shot and shooter glasses are endless. You can buy necklace shot glasses, shot glass rings, test tube shots, glasses that light up, and glasses that are split in two so you can pour one spirit on one side of the divider and something else on the other. They can also be found in practically any shape imaginable, such as boots, bullets, body parts, animals, and cacti. Edible shot glasses can be made, and glasses made of chocolate, candy, gummy bears, or ice or any liquid that will freeze can be bought. You can even find checker-

Shot and Shooter Glasses

- A shot glass will measure 1–2 ounces.

- Shot glasses are available in a variety of shapes and sizes.

- A shooter glass will measure 2–5 ounces.

- Shooter glasses can be found in many shapes and sizes, too.

Pony and Cordial Glasses

- In bar terms, the word *pony* is a unit of measurement of 1 ounce, so pony glasses will always measure 1 ounce.

- Pony glasses are always stemmed.

- Cordial glasses can range in size from 1 ounce to 3 ounces.

- A serving of cordial or liqueur would be served in a cordial glass.

boards and chessboards that use shot and shooter glasses.

Sometimes pony and cordial glasses are used for shot and shooter glasses, but bars don't seem to carry them anymore because they get stolen. You'll find that they're used domestically for nice dinner parties. A pony glass is a cordial glass, but not all cordial glasses can be called "pony glasses" because of their measurement. All liqueurs and cordials such as crèmes, creams, and schnapps can be poured into cordial glasses.

ZOOM

On the rocks is a popular bar term that means to pour the spirit over ice. That's how the rocks glass gets its name. Something on the rocks will have spirit only. You can have anything on the rocks that you desire, but the most popular choices are whiskey, Scotch, Amaretto, and Irish cream.

Rocks Glasses

- Rocks glasses should measure 5–7 ounces.

- Rocks glasses are meant to hold a portion of spirit without mixer over ice.

- Rocks glasses come in a variety of shapes and sizes.

- Shooters are often strained into rocks glasses.

The Largest and Most Valuable

Brad Rodgers holds the Guinness world record for the largest shot glass collection. He lives in Las Vegas and has around twelve thousand shot glasses, but three thousand of them are duplicates, so those don't count. Guinness has him on record as owning almost nine thousand shot glasses. The most valuable shot glasses are the official glasses of the Kentucky Derby.

THE STURDIEST GLASSWARE
Strong and steady glassware can be handled firmly

A lot of bar glassware requires a delicate touch or else a stem will snap or the lip will chip. You still have to care for the glassware discussed on this page, but most can be handled quite roughly with little wear and tear.

Basically, these glasses are just slightly different from each other in size and measurement. The Highball has been around since the 1800s. Its name more than likely came from standing tall at medium height. There are a couple of stories about

its origin. One is that the Highball is a drink before dinner when the sun is a big ball in the sky. Another is that the Highball came from the railroad practice of raising a ball quickly on a pole. The most popular Highballs are Scotch and Soda, Gin and Tonic, Bourbon and Coke, and Seven and Seven.

Often bars will stock old-fashioned glasses and call them their "highball glasses." What they mean is that they make their Highballs in old-fashioned glasses, but most people

Highball Glasses

- Highball glasses should measure 7–10 ounces.

- A highball consists of one spirit and one mixer.

- Originally a Highball was a drink made of rye whiskey and ginger ale over ice.

- Today the traditional medium-tall highball glass is not used in bars often. Instead bars use an old-fashioned glass, so the names of the glasses get interchanged all the time.

Old-fashioned Glasses

- Old-fashioned glasses should measure 7–12 ounces.

- These glasses are shorter and squattier than traditional highball glasses.

- They are sometimes referred to as "lowball glasses"

- because the height of the glass is lower but used for a Highball cocktail.

- These glasses get their name from the cocktail that was originally made in them, called an "old fashioned."

don't know the difference. The double old-fashioned glass is excellent for when you want a double.

A Collins glass is named after the drink Tom Collins. Traditional Collins glasses are frosted with a clear lip.

ZOOM

The 1938 film *Jezebel* starring Bette Davis is set in New Orleans in 1852. The first scene shows a man pulling his carriage next to the Louis-House to *have a ball*, as he says. It's assumed that he means a Highball because the next scene shows him and other gentlemen standing and drinking at an elegant lobby bar.

GLASSWARE

These glasses hold more than the old-fashioned glasses

Double Old-fashioned Glasses

- These glasses are larger than old-fashioned glasses.

- A double old-fashioned glass can measure 12–15 ounces.

- Most men prefer to have their drinks in a short, sturdy glass instead of a tall one, so this glass works well for this purpose.

- This glass is also called a "bucket" in some parts of America.

Tall and Collins Glasses

- The Collins glass is a tall, straight-sided glass that can measure 10–12 ounces.

- A Collins glass is also called a "chimney glass" because of its shape.

- A tall glass in the cocktail world can measure 10–20 ounces.

- Tall glasses are available in a variety of colors and shapes.

THE STEMMED GLASSWARE
Learn the different uses for this tall and elegant stemware

The cocktail glass symbolizes the cocktail culture. The cocktail glass was fairly small, usually 4–7 ounces, until around the millennium. It was around that time that the martini craze took over. Froufrou fruity martinis required more mixers, so the glass had no choice but to become larger. These millennium martinis can be made in a tall glass with ice, but when strained into elegant and sexy glasses they seem more appealing and fun. The downside is that that much liquid without ice warms up pretty fast, especially when you are touching it with your hands.

The margarita glass with the salt, ice, and lime in the photo is supposed to resemble a sombrero. You also can look for some Mexican glass margarita glasses to be truly authentic.

When you see a hurricane glass, you should think of Pat O'Brien's and New Orleans in the 1930s because that's where it originated. Today in New Orleans hurricane glasses are ev-

Cocktail Glasses

- Cocktail glasses can measure 4–12 ounces.

- These glasses are the icon of the cocktail world.

- All martini glasses are cocktail glasses, but not all cocktail glasses are martini glasses.

- The cocktail determines the size of the glass to be used.

Margarita Glasses

- Margarita glasses can measure 8–16 ounces.

- Because margaritas can be served straight up, on the rocks, or frozen, there is a variety of glassware to choose from.

- Some bars use an all-purpose glass like a pint glass for 90 percent of their drinks, and a margarita will be served in that.

- Mexican restaurants usually carry authentic margarita glasses.

erywhere and are available in every color imaginable, but the most prized is the souvenir glass at Pat O'Brien's. It's a 26-ounce glass with the Pat O'Brien's logo. It will hold $10 in pennies.

ZOOM

The Bombay Sapphire gin company holds a yearly designer martini glass competition. The martini glasses that are created by designer students from around the world will leave you breathless. One winner from each country competes in a final competition. The showcase of glasses can be viewed in person each year by attending the world-touring Bombay Sapphire Blue Room exhibition.

Hurricane Glasses

- Hurricane glasses can measure 12–26 ounces.

- They are often used as a festive souvenir glass and are plentiful in plastic and glass.

- Some bars will invest in hurricane glasses and use them as their frozen and tropical drink glasses.

- The shape of the glass came from the shape of a hurricane lamp.

Poco Grande Glasses

- Poco grande glasses can measure 10–13 ounces.

- Stems on a poco grande can vary in shape, but the curvy shape of the bowl will stay the same.

- Some call this glass a "tulip glass."

- This is also a glass that some bars will dedicate for their frozen and tropical drinks if they make the investment.

THE SPECIALTY GLASSWARE

Historic specialty glassware is still used today

In France during the 1800s, the absinthe glass was served on a saucer. Most establishments had their logo imprinted on the saucers, and patrons would stack them neatly on the table. When they were finished, their bar tab was calculated by how many saucers were stacked.

Modern tiki mugs exploded and flourished in the golden age of tiki, which was between 1933 and 1973. There were tiki bars, lounges, and rooms with a wide assortment of ex-

otic tropical drinks on their menus. A tiki drink was usually accompanied by extravagant garnishes and decorations, such as paper umbrellas, Chinese back scratchers, tropical flowers, sugarcane sticks, dry ice to create mist, and fruit and more fruit. Tiki mugs are in a world all their own. You find tiki skulls, Easter Island heads, fruit-shaped mugs, volcano mugs, barrels, figures, and more!

The most expensive mint julep sells for $1,000 at the Ken-

Absinthe Glasses

- Absinthe glasses can measure 7–10 ounces.

- Absinthe glasses come in a variety of shapes and sizes, but they almost always have an ornate quality to them.

- The price range of an absinthe glass can be $10–$1,000.

- Some absinthe glasses have built-in reservoirs so you can pour the exact amount of liqueur into the glass without measuring.

Irish Coffee Glasses

- Irish coffee glasses should measure 6-10 ounces. Anymore, and the alcohol portion will need to be adjusted

- These glasses are available in a variety of colored glass, but clear is the most often used.

- There are two basic styles: the footed glass mug with a handle and the stemmed bowl.

- You can serve an Irish coffee in this glass, but all other hot and warm bar drinks are served in this glass as well.

tucky Derby. Every year Woodford Reserve Bourbon sells "millionaire mint juleps" for charity. Sometimes the ingredients are local, and sometimes Brown-Forman (the company that owns the bourbon) spans the globe to collect mint from Aspen or Ireland, sugar from Australia or South America, and ice from icebergs or the Bavarian Alps. The juleps are served in gold-plated cups with silver straws.

Tiki Mugs

- Tiki mugs can measure 7–20 ounces.

- Over thirty varieties of tiki mugs are available in many shapes and sizes.

- The word *tiki* refers to a carved statue of a Polynesian god.

- Tiki mugs are usually ceramic and made by slip casting in a plaster mold, then dried, glazed, and fired in a kiln.

Mint Julep Cups

- Mint julep cups can measure 6–12 ounces.

- You can serve a mint julep in a variety of glasses, but the silver cup is the traditional way to serve it.

- A silver or pewter cup helps coat the outside with frost.

- Thousands of mint julep cups and glasses abound in Louisville the first week of May because of the Kentucky Derby.

MIXERS 1
Learn the basics of the most common mixers

In July 2008, New Orleans became the first city in America to be granted an official cocktail by the Louisiana legislature. The cocktail granted was the Sazerac. The Sazerac was invented in the early 1800s, and the recipe calls for Peychaud's (pronounced pay-SHOWDS) bitters. About 90 percent of employed bartenders reading these words know of only one bitters that sits behind their bar: Angostura. And they probably pick it up only to jerk a few dashes into soda water

to drink for a stomachache. Occasionally they may use it to make a Manhattan or Old Fashioned or to soak some sugar cubes for some Champagne cocktails. Well, I'm here to tell you that bitters has made a comeback and is a staple among modern mixologists worldwide. Some are making their own bitters! Bitters that has been dead for one hundred plus years and found in historic cocktail books is being revived. Regan's Orange Bitters No. 6 is a great example of the revived orange

Bitters

- The first known definition of the word *cocktail* listed bitters as one of the ingredients in the recipe. The year was 1806.

- Bitters is a concentrated witches' brew of herbs, roots, seeds, alcohol, and more.

- Bitters does not make a drink taste bitter. It adds a punch of flavor to cocktails.

- The most popular bitters that has lasted the test of time is Angostura.

Juice Mixers

- Juice provides four elements in a cocktail: sweetness, color, texture, and flavor.

- Juices used for cocktails should be as fresh and pure as possible.

- Juice can derive from fruit or vegetables.

- The most common juices found behind most bars are orange, grapefruit, cranberry, and pineapple. Since the millennium you will also find lemon, lime, pomegranate, and white cranberry juice.

bitters that so many recipe books call for. It was invented by cocktail and spirits expert Gary Regan. Fee Brothers (a four-generation-old manufacturer of quality cocktail mixes) now has seven bitters: lemon, orange, mint, peach, whiskey barrel aged, grapefruit, and old fashioned. So, get bitter!

Sweet Mixers

- Sweetness can play a very important role in cocktails.

- Simple syrup (sugar and water) is the most common sweetener used in a cocktail.

- A sweetener like grenadine can add color as well as sweetness.

- Other cocktail sweeteners include maraschino and hibiscus syrup, coconut cream, flavored syrups, liqueurs and cordials, maple syrup, honey, gomme, orgeat, purees, and lime cordial (like Rose's Lime Juice).

Dairy Mixers

- Cream can be used for cocktails, but most bars carry half-and-half (half milk, half cream).

- Soy milk can be substituted as an eco-milk or cream.

- High-end bars make their own fresh whipped cream instead of using the canned aerosol.

- More dairy mixers include ice cream, yogurt, unsalted butter, eggnog, and eggs.

MIXERS & GARNISHES

MIXERS 2
A second round of mixers can be added to your cocktail repertoire

The most overlooked cocktail ingredient is ice. Ice is not just for chilling a cocktail. The dilution melts into a cocktail and changes the taste, especially if the ice machine you are using does not have a filter! If the ice machine makes ice from a city tap water line, then you are diluting chlorine and other contaminants into your cocktail. Cocktail ice should be made with filtered water and its size should be large for minimal dilution. Machines that make square-inch cubes are ideal. How

many times have you ordered a cocktail at a bar, and within one minute the wafer-thin kitchen ice was already melted halfway up the glass? Bars and restaurants that respect cocktails install a second ice machine that makes big, beautiful cocktail ice.

Bloody Marys are adaptable enough to withstand a myriad of mixers added to them. One extra ingredient I've been using for years in addition to the Worcestershire sauce is a

Coffee, Tea, or Cocktail?

Coffee has been a mixer for alcoholic drinks for a very long time. The most famous is Irish coffee. Many restaurants and bars even have coffee drink menus. Typically these drinks are ordered as after-dinner drinks. Around the millennium, espresso made its way into cocktails, and modern bartenders love experimenting with tea-based cocktails.

Water-based Mixers

- The most important water-based mixer for a cocktail is water itself.

- Ice plays an extremely important role in a cocktail.

- When you shake, stir, or serve a cocktail with ice, the

- melting ice is considered an essential part of the cocktail.

- Other water-based mixers include coffee, espresso, tea, and dry mixers mixed with water such as cider or chocolate.

little bit of A-1 steak sauce. Most people don't know that I've mixed a little into their drink and always comment on how good the Bloody Mary tastes.

A small grater works well for grating fresh nutmeg. One can be found for about $10.

Savory Mixers

- The most common savory mixers are hot sauces, Worcestershire sauce, beef bouillon, steak sauce, Clamato juice, and clam juice.

- Clamato and clam juice are very popular in Canada.

- Popular cocktails made with savory ingredients include the Bloody Mary, Bloody Bull, Bloody Caesar, Bloody Maria, Red Eye, and Prairie Fire.

- These ingredients can be mixed before or stirred in after.

Dry Mixers

- Dry mixers used for cocktails include salt, celery salt, chili pepper, cayenne pepper, white pepper, cocoa powder, cloves, cinnamon, spicy seasonings, powdered hot chocolate, and powdered apple cider.

- Dry mixers can be added at anytime in the cocktail-making process.

- Often dry mixers are sprinkled on top of a cocktail.

- Always try to use the freshest ingredients possible.

CUTTING WEDGES & WHEELS

Grab some citrus and a sharp knife and learn to cut your first garnish

A sharp knife is crucial when cutting garnishes. A dull knife is dangerous because it can slip off the food you're cutting and cut your fingers instead. Serrated knives have little teeth that can grab hold of citrus fruit better for beginners, and they don't need sharpening. You can keep other knives sharpened by using a long rod called *steel* or other types of knife sharpeners.

Always make sure your hands, the knife, and what you are cutting are dry before you start cutting. When you come to a stage of cutting when the blade is getting too close to your fingers, simply curl them under while still applying firm pressure.

Wheels for drink garnishes are very decorative. However, they are not practical to squeeze into a drink because of the mess doing so will make on your hands. Wedges are designed to be easily lifted off the edge of a drink and then

Wheels: Step 1

- Wheels can be cut from any fruit or vegetable with a circular shape. The most common is citrus.

- For this demonstration, a lemon is used.

- 1. Begin with a secure, clean surface. Cut off the end of the lemons.

- 2. Make a ¼-inch slice into the lengthwise part of the lemon. This slice allows the wheel to rest on the rim of a glass.

Wheels: Step 2

- 1. Hold the lemon firmly down with one hand.

- 2. Carefully slice the width of the lemon into wheels.

- If you need to make several wheels or desire very thin

- wheels, use a kitchen slicer or mandolin.

- If the wheels will not be used to set on a rim, then you can skip step 2 in the previous photo.

squeezed to add flavor in one smooth motion. Some people cut off the ends of a piece of fruit and then cut wedges, but I don't like that amputated dogtail dock look because you lose the beautiful curve of the fruit. And when you squeeze it, your fingers touch the meat of the fruit.

Wedges: Step 1

- Wedges can be cut from any fruit or vegetable with a circular shape. The most common is citrus.

- For this demonstration, we are using a lime.

- 1. Begin with a secure, clean surface, then slice the lime in half lengthwise.

- 2. Make a ¼-inch slice into the meat of the lime widthwise. This slice allows the wedge to rest on the rim of a glass.

Wedges: Step 2

- 1. Hold the lime firmly down with one hand.

- 2. Carefully slice the length of the lime at an angle.

- Each half lime should yield three or four wedges.

- If the wedges will not be used to set on a rim, then you can skip step 2 in the previous photo.

MAKING TWISTS
C'mon, take a spoon and a knife in your hand and do the twist!

The bar term *twist* refers to a thin strip of lemon rind that is twisted over a cocktail to release its oils, then gently rubbed around the rim of the glass so that the pungent citrus oil can be tasted when taking a drink. A twist is the thicker and sturdier brother of a lemon zest, and often the two words are used interchangeably.

One twist that is often confusing to bartenders and guests is the lime wedge twist. I believe that the practice of calling a wedge of lime a "twist" came about because TV and film writers did not know the difference. Typically people will order a soda water *with a twist*. What they really want is a soda water with a wedge of lime.

The most popular drinks that a lemon twist *can be* used for are classic martinis (think James Bond), a whiskey neat or on the rocks, and a cup of espresso. The recent resurrection of the Sazerac calls for a lemon twist, but the twist is not dropped

Twists: Step 1

- 1. Cut the ends off a lemon.

- 2. Slip a spoon between the rind and the meat, then run it around the lemon on both ends.

- The goal is to separate the meat from the rind.

- Another way is to make a lengthwise slice in the rind, then separate the rind and meat with your fingertips or spoon.

Twists: Step 2

- 1. Vertically slice the whole rind once. Or, if you prefer, you can lay the rind on its side and make one slice.

- This slice is the lengthwise slice you'd be making in the other way using your fingertips or spoon.

- Make sure to save the lemon meat for juicing.

into the cocktail. The reason why I say that a lemon twist *can be* used is because it's something that a guest will request. It's not part of the recipe like in the Sazerac. And that brings me to talk a little about cocktail garnishes. Garnishes are meant to enhance a cocktail either by taste or appearance. A garnish should tell you something about the ingredients in the drink. For example, a drink with pineapple juice could be garnished with a pineapple slice. If candied ginger is part of a garnish, then I would assume that there's something "ginger" in the

cocktail. Guests can choose not to eat the garnish and set it aside on a cocktail napkin or push it into the drink.

Be extra careful when working with slippery rinds.

Twists: Step 3

- 1. Tightly roll up the lemon rind.

- 2. Secure the rolled rind with a bamboo or toothpick by pushing it all the way through the rind.

- Securing the rind makes the next step of slicing easier.

- Some people don't secure the rind and just hold it tightly with their fingers. It can be done but be warned of its slip factor.

Twists: Step 4

- 1. Slice the secured rolled rind to make twists.

- An average lemon can yield up to eight twists.

- Fatter lemons make for longer twists.

- Another way to make twists is to cut lengthwise strips around a lemon, then cut off one end. You can now pull off a twist as you need one. However, these will be shorter.

CUTTING A PINEAPPLE

Learn to cut America's most exotic fruit to slip a new trick up your sleeve

Of all the garnishes I show people how to cut into slices, the pineapple is always their favorite. It seems that they feel they just learned a cool new trick like making a balloon animal or whistling by placing two fingers into their mouth. Whatever the reason, know that you will need a larger space than normal when cutting a pineapple. And a larger knife.

You can also save the top end of the pineapple (with the fronds). It can be used as decoration in a display or bamboo-skewered fruit kebabs could stick into it. The fronds can also be torn off and used as a garnish. You'll have to trim the bottoms of them a little for the sake of visual presentation. You can also spear fronds on a pineapple slice. A fancy way to

Cutting a Pineapple: Step 1

- 1. Begin with a secure, clean surface.

- 2. Slice off the ends of a pineapple.

- 3. Carefully cut the pineapple in half lengthwise.

- 4. Discard the ends.

Cutting a Pineapple: Step 2

- 1. Lay the pineapple halves flat for cutting stability.

- 2. Slice both pineapple halves lengthwise.

- The result will be four lengthwise pineapple quarters.

- After some practice, you may discover that you prefer to cut the quarters in half to make eighths. This will yield more slices in the end.

attach the fronds to a pineapple slice is to make an incision in the top of the slice, then insert a couple of fronds down into the incision point side up. For punches made with pineapple juice, just throw a handful of fronds in for fun.

Drinks that could get a pineapple slice garnish are Piña Colada, Bay Breeze, Planter's Punch, Singapore Sling, or any tropical drink made with pineapple juice.

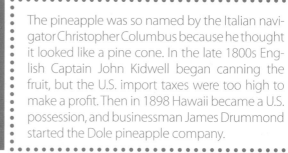

The pineapple was so named by the Italian navigator Christopher Columbus because he thought it looked like a pine cone. In the late 1800s English Captain John Kidwell began canning the fruit, but the U.S. import taxes were too high to make a profit. Then in 1898 Hawaii became a U.S. possession, and businessman James Drummond started the Dole pineapple company.

Cutting a Pineapple: Step 3

- 1. Firmly hold down a pineapple quarter (because the outside curve of the pineapple is unstable). Make a careful ½-inch lengthwise slice into a pineapple quarter.

- 2. This slice allows the slice to rest on the rim of a glass.

- 3. Repeat with the other three pineapple quarters.

- 4. The result will be four lengthwise pineapple quarters with rim slices.

Cutting a Pineapple: Step 4

- 1. Turn the pineapple quarter on its flat, stable side, then hold firmly.

- 2. Make many slices widthwise.

- 3. Repeat with the other three pineapple quarters.

- 4. The result should be 30–40 pineapple slices that will rest on the rim of a glass.

ADDITIONAL GARNISHES
Discover the ever-growing world of cocktail garnishes

The top four garnishes every bar will have are lemons, limes, olives, and maraschino cherries. From that foundation a tower of garnishes can be built. Next in line would be oranges, pineapples, strawberries, and mint.

There's really no limit when it comes to garnishes. Some bars carry nontypical garnishes because of their signature cocktail menu. These can include peaches, grapes, mango, wild hibiscus flowers, orchids, rose petals, berries, pears, ap-

ples, kiwi, watermelon, cantaloupe, bananas, basil, rosemary, sugared ginger, and sugarcane sticks.

Unusual garnishes in this book are chocolate-covered strawberries, chocolate-dipped fortune cookies, lychees, rims of Pop Rocks, edible gold, crushed cookies, crushed candy, coconut flakes, celery salt, a frosted doughnut, red wax lips, gummy worms, flowers, and black string licorice.

Nonedible additions to a drink are called "decorations" and

Making Flags

- Originally a flag was an orange slice that was speared with a cherry.

- Today a flag is anything that has been speared with a cherry.

- You can cut and spear the fruit anyway your heart desires.

- Look for fun and interesting cocktail picks to make flags.

Stuffing Olives

- 1. To make stuffed olives, first buy some large, green olives, preferably without the pimentos. If you can find only pimento-stuffed olives, simply remove the pimentos.

- 2. Now stuff with your chosen ingredients.

- Olives can be stuffed with practically anything you like.

- Some popular stuffing choices are blue cheese (or any cheese), whole almonds, garlic, pearl onions, and jalapeños.

"tools." Sometimes the decorations can serve as a tool, such as a paper parasol speared with a cherry. There are unlimited choices when it comes to straws, picks, and stir sticks.

Some drinks automatically get a certain garnish. Limes are used for Margaritas, tonics (Gin and Tonic and so forth), Cape Codders, and Cuba Libres. Lemons are used for teas (Long Island, Long Beach, and so forth), and orange flags are used for sours (Tom Collins, Whiskey Sour, and so forth).

MAKE IT EASY

Get creative with your Bloody Marys! For example, why not make a pizza Bloody Mary? Rim one half with Parmesan cheese and the other half with chili pepper sprinkles or a combination of both. Garnish with a skewer of pepperoni slices, cheese cubes, and olives. If you like Hawaiian pizza, then put pineapple and ham cubes onto the skewer.

Bloody Mary Garnishes

- The Bloody Mary has the largest assortment of possible garnishes to choose from.

- Try spearing garnishes on a celery stalk.

- Generally, a Bloody Mary gets a lime wedge, and if it is made with plain tomato juice, it gets a lemon wedge.

- Some restaurants set up a self-service Bloody Mary table filled with a wide assortment of garnishes, hot sauces, and spices.

Ideas for Bloody Mary Garnishes

Bloody Mary garnishes can include celery, pickles, pickled okra, pickled green beans, olives (green, black, stuffed), peppers (green, yellow, red, pepperoncini), limes, lemons, tomatoes (cherry, grape, plum), onions (green, raw rings, cocktail), asparagus, baby corn, mushrooms, carrot sticks, cucumbers (sticks or rounds), avocado slices, peel-and-eat shrimp, radishes, cheese cubes, Slim Jims, salted rim, and celery salt rim.

BEER & GLASSWARE

Pull up a stool and learn about the most historic alcohol of all

As far as historians know, beer was the first documented alcoholic beverage. Archaeologists have found million-year-old grapevine fossils, but unless there is documented proof, then it simply doesn't count. Recipes for beer have been found on ninety-two Babylonian stone tablets, in residue from nine thousand-year-old Chinese pottery, in Egyptian and Turkish tombs, and on many European cave walls.

Today beer-drinking vessels are mostly made of glass. The stein is the most decorative beer glass of them all. It was invented in the 1300s, and by the 1500s lids were attached to keep out the flies. In modern times steins are mostly bought for a tourist souvenir or for a collection. The yard glass is the largest beer glass. Basically, it's 1 yard in length and can hold 1.14 liters of beer. Beer is also the only alcoholic beverage available in many packages: bottles, cans, kegs, or casks.

There are over twenty thousand brands of beer worldwide,

Beer Glasses

- Beer glasses can measure 12–42 ounces.

- Beer has the most types of glassware: around twenty.

- The three most common all-beer glasses are the pint, pilsner, and mug.

- There is a variety of pilsner glasses, but all are thin at the bottom and wider at the top.

Ales

- Ale was the first beer ever recorded.

- The first ales were sweet, murky, thick, and warm.

- Hops were not introduced to ales until the 1400s. Until that time, ales used an herb mixture called "gruit."

- Ale types include stout, porter, wheat, bitter, lambic, brown, cream, and pale.

and all of those beers fall under only two categories: ale or lager. Ales use top-fermenting yeast, and lagers use bottom-fermenting yeast.

Before the 1980s, beer—for the most part— was just guzzled. It was at this time that small craft beers and microbreweries began popping up, a movement that showed an appreciation for the art of the brew.

Lagers

- In 1842, the first golden pilsner was invented in Pilzen, Czech (now called Czech Republic) by Josef Groll. It is called "Pilsner Urquell."

- Adolphus Busch was the first U.S. brewer to use pasteurization to keep lager fresh.

- Adolphus Busch was the first to use refrigerated railroad cars in 1876. Budweiser was shipped from coast to coast.

- Lager types include bock, dry, light, pilsner, ice, malt, amber, and export.

Beer Trivia

- The Mayflower pilgrims planned to sail farther but ran out of beer at Plymouth Rock, so the decision was made to disembark.

- Oktoberfest was first celebrated in 1810 in Munich, Germany.

- The New York Public Library has a piece of notebook paper bearing a beer recipe written by George Washington in 1757.

FRUIT & BARLEY

RED WINE & GLASSWARE
Learn the basics of red wine through the grapevine

Walking through a forest of wine bottles at your local store can be overwhelming. Yes, there is a lot to know about wine, and entire books have been written on wine, but I hope to help you understand the basics.

Wine is made from fermented fruit, and the most popular fruit used is grapes. Its history spans thousands of years through every civilization. Today's top wine-producing countries are France, America, Australia, Spain, Italy, and Argentina.

All wines basically are one of two styles: red or white. These styles break down into three body types: full, medium, and light. Even though there are over ten thousand types of grapes in the world, only about three hundred of these are used to make commercial wine. Out of these three hundred, twenty to thirty are used for the most popular wines. In the wine world, you will hear the word *varietal* often. This refers to the type of grape used. Popular red (and black) wine grapes

Red Wine Glasses

- Red wine glasses have a round, wide bowl. A proper serving is 5–6 ounces.

- The largeness of the bowl allows more room for the wine to breathe.

- Some modern red wine glasses offer curvier op-

tions, but the opening will never be larger than the bowl.

- A glass of red wine is held with the fingertips touching the bottom of the bowl because warming the wine is not an issue.

Full-bodied Red Wines

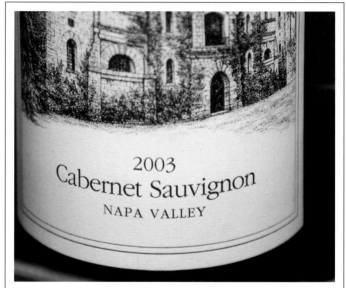

2003
Cabernet Sauvignon
NAPA VALLEY

- Full-bodied (sometimes called "heavy-bodied") wines are very dark in color, have a heavy feel on the tongue, and are high in tannins.

- The king grape of heavy-bodied wine is the Cabernet Sauvignon grape.

- Other popular full-bodied red wines include Bordeaux, Malbec, and Burgundy.

- Full-bodied wines are usually too strong for the beginner and are something to be graduated to.

used to make red wine include Cabernet Sauvignon, Merlot, Pinot Noir, Sangiovese, Shiraz/Syrah, Zinfandel, Gamay, Grenache, Lambrusco, Pinot Meunier, and Tempranillo.

Wine stores and wine sections are always organized for you (normally by country). After you narrow down the country, then you can narrow down the body type of wine you prefer and/or the varietal (grape) you prefer. Wine labels will give you all the information you need to know about the wine: location of the vineyard, vintage (year the grapes were harvested), varietal (grape type), brand name, and producer of the wine.

Some countries have label laws that require a government warning, alcohol content, and the list of sulfites used.

Also know that varietals are often blended together, so it's not uncommon to find a Cabernet-Shiraz or a Cabernet-Merlot mix.

Medium-bodied Red Wines

- Medium-bodied red wines will not be as intense as full-bodied red wines in the mouth.

- The color of a medium-bodied wine will be lighter than that of a full-bodied red wine and darker than that of a light-bodied wine.

- A fruity taste is found with a medium-bodied wine.

- Popular medium-bodied red wines include Merlot, Shiraz/Syrah, Chianti, and some Pinot Noirs.

Light-bodied Red Wines

- Light-bodied red wines are ruby red in color and often referred to as "table wines."

- This type of wine is good for beginners because of its light and fruity taste and feel on the tongue.

- The Gamay grape is a popular grape for light-bodied red wines.

- Popular light-bodied red wines include Beaujolais, Lambrusco, and some Pinot Noirs.

WHITE WINE & GLASSWARE
Discover the best butter- and straw-colored sweet or dry chilled vino

The first thing to know about white wine is that it can be made from white, red, purple, or even black grapes. This is because the grape skins are discarded when making white wine. With red wine, the skins are not discarded. And for pink-toned wines like White Zinfandel, Rosé, or Blush, the skins are left on just a little bit to color the wine.

Just like red wines, white wines will vary in body. They will also vary from dryness to sweetness. Popular grapes to make white wine include Chardonnay, Sauvignon Blanc, Chenin Blanc, Pinot Gris/Pinot Grigio, Pinot Blanc, Gewürztraminer, Riesling, and Viognier. All of these white wine varietals can have a dry or super sweet taste because it all depends on who grows the grapes.

Growing grapes to make wine is indeed an artform. So many elements determined by nature and determined by people come into play. Grapevines love warm, dry summers

White Wine Glasses

- The shape of a white wine glass is narrow. A proper measure is 5–6 ounces.

- White wine glasses are held at the stem to avoid warming the wine.

- Restaurants and bars dedicated to the art of wine will carry both a white wine glass and a red wine glass.

- Most establishments will carry an all-purpose wine glass for both types of wine.

Full-bodied White Wine

- The full-bodied Chardonnay grape is the queen of the white grapes.

- The Chardonnay grape is the most popular white wine grape in California. It's also one of the grapes used to make Champagne.

- Chardonnay is heavy, buttery, fruity, and oaky.

- Some winemakers don't like the oakiness of Chardonnay, so they age the wine in stainless steel tanks.

and mild winters. Who doesn't? And all grape varietals have a favorite soil. For example, Riesling grapes love a slate-rich soil, and Chardonnay grapes love limestone. Plant each other in their opposing soils, and it would be disastrous! Other factors that come into play are sun exposure, bugs, rainfall, drainage, and more.

Medium-bodied White Wine

- Medium-bodied white wine is a lighter color than the heavy-bodied Chardonnay.

- Popular medium-bodied white wines include Viognier, Pinot Blanc, and Gewürztraminer.

- Sauvignon Blanc (also called "Fume Blanc") is probably the best example of a medium-bodied white wine.

- Sauvignon Blanc has a dry, grassy, citrus, crisp taste.

Light-bodied White Wine

- Light-bodied white wine is the lightest in color.

- The Riesling grape originated in Germany and is Germany's leading grape varietal. Most productions have a light, sweet taste.

- Popular light-bodied white wines include Chenin Blanc and Pinot Gris/Pinot Grigio.

- Light-bodied wines are often drunk in the summer or at a picnic.

FRUIT & BARLEY

CHAMPAGNE & GLASSWARE

Explore the most celebratory liquid of all time

Ironically, in modern times we adore and celebrate the fifty million bubbles in a bottle of Champagne, but until the mid-1600s, bubbles in a bottle of wine meant that the winemaker had failed. The proof was in a wine-soaked cellar full of burst bottles. Locals referred to this wine as "demon" or "devil wine." It's funny how things change with time.

Many people believe that a blind French monk named "Dom Pérignon" invented Champagne, but the fact is that Champagne invented itself. This is because the Champagne region is in northern France. That means that that part of France has a short growing season (due to being colder) and that the harvest season ends up being in the late autumn. The coldness of winter stops the fermentation inside the bottles, then when springs rolls around the fermentation picks up where it left off and creates bubbles inside the bottle. Dom can most definitely be credited for *improving* Champagne because

Champagne Glasses

- There are basically two types of Champagne glasses: the coupe (or saucer) and the flute. Five ounces is a proper serving.

- The flute is broken down into two other types called "trumpet" and "tulip."

- The trumpet has a shape flared up and out, and the tulip has curvy variations.

- The flute-type Champagne glass is meant to keep the bubbles fresher.

Champagne

- Unlike most other wines, Champagnes are named after the houses that produce them.

- Champagnes come in levels from sweet to dry: Doux, Demi-Sec, Sec, Extra Dry, Brut, Brut Zero, Ultra Brut, and Extra Brut.

- A good temperature to serve Champagne is 44°F.

- Only three grapes are used to make Champagne: Pinot Noir, Pinot Meunier, and Chardonnay.

his passion was to figure out a way to keep the bottles from exploding. And he did. He found thicker and stronger bottles made in England, used Spanish-inspired cork stoppers instead of wood stoppers, and created a blending of black grapes grown in the Champagne region called "cuvée."

Sparkling Wine

Prosecco

- The reason why there is even a category of sparkling wine is because of the Champagne Riots in the early 1900s.

- The Champagne Riots resulted in a law requiring that only Champagne made with grapes in the Champagne region could bear the word *Champagne* on their label.

- The words *sparkling wine* can be seen on all bottles of sparkling wine made after 1927.

- Prosecco is a grape used to make Italian sparkling wine.

- The prosecco grape is prized for its delicate flavors and aromatic taste and flavor.

- The most famous cocktail made with prosecco is the Bellini (white peach puree and prosecco).

- In 2006, Paris Hilton released a trendy lifestyle beverage in a can that is a mixture of prosecco and artificial flavorings called "Rich Prosecco."

FRUIT & BARLEY

PORT, SHERRY, & GLASSWARE
Learn about the other wine-based choices that are steeped deep in history

Making sherry isn't as cut and dried as making port. With port, winemakers just add brandy to prematurely stop the fermentation of the wine, then age it. Sherry is made with the solera system, which is a time-consuming blending of older wines and younger wines little by little by hand while they're aging in the barrels. The wines are also exposed to air

as they're aging, which is monitored. Another difference is that sherry is fortified with a grape-based spirit, but brandy is not. However, there is one difficult factor about port, and that is the growing conditions of the grapes. The vineyards are located on remote, steep slopes that drop down to the Douro River in Portugal. It is by far the most difficult wine-growing

Port and Sherry Glasses

- A proper serving of port or sherry is 2½–3 ounces.

- A port glass is like a miniature wine glass. It's always stemmed with a nicely shaped bowl.

- Port and sherry glasses are the older siblings of cordial glasses.

- Port and sherry are often accompanied with a cigar after dinner. Some smokers dip their cigars into the wine.

Port

- True port is made in the Douro River valley in northern Portugal. Today other countries make versions of it.

- Port types are tawny (dry) and ruby (sweet).

- The word *port* is short for the name of the port town of Oporto, not Portugal.

- Port was the first fortified wine made by adding brandy to it and then aging.

region in the world. Both sherry and port have a rich history because they could be carried on long sea voyages without spoiling. England is credited with making port popular because in the seventeenth century the English were not allowed any French wines due to trade wars, so they turned to Portugal.

Madeira, too, has a rich history. Just like port and sherry, it was stocked on ships bound for extended voyages. However, an interesting accident occurred with the barrels of Madeira. While being exposed to the extreme heat of sailing near the equator, instead of spoiling the Madeira, the heat actually baked a soft, burnt richness into the fortified wine. At the time, Madeira seemed magical and intriguing. It was the wine used to toast the signing of the Declaration of Independence, and the U.S.S. *Constitution* was christened with a bottle of Madeira. Today winemakers heat the barrels at 100–140°F for several months to simulate the extreme tropic heat.

Sherry

- Sherry is made only in and around the triangular area of the town of Jerez, Spain.

- Sherry comes in two types: fino (dry and light) and oloroso (sweet and dark).

- Fino comes in three styles: Fino, Manzanilla, and Amontillado. Oloroso also comes in three styles: Oloroso, Cream, and Pedro Ximenez.

- Finos are drunk chilled and the olorosos at room temperature. Cooking sherry is not for drinking.

Madeira and Vermouth

- Madeira is wine fortified with grape brandy and made on Madeira Island, Portugal.

- The four types of Madeira are Malvasia, Bual, Verdelho, and Sercial.

- Vermouth is a fortified white wine that has a spirit (usually brandy) added, then is aromatized with herbs and botanicals such as seeds, plants, and flowers.

- Vermouth comes in two types: dry (white) and sweet (red). Pictured is domestic vermouth. For superior cocktails, buy French dry or Italian sweet.

BRANDY, COGNAC, & GLASSWARE
What do apples, grapes, kings, and presidents have in common?

Applejack brandy is as American as apple pie or cherry trees. Laird's Applejack was the first commercial distillery in America, and records show a written request by the first president, George Washington, asking for the applejack recipe. How about them apples?

For centuries, the brandy called "cognac" has been the king of brandies. And cognac has been the choice of kings. The king of cognac is even named after a king. It's called "King Louis the XIII," and Remy Martin produces it. It's aged for forty to one hundred years in French oak barrels that are several hundred years old, and it's packaged in a Baccarat crystal bottle. The price of a bottle starts at $1,500.

The term *angel's share* or *angel's portion* refers to the 3 percent evaporation of cognac as it ages in wooden casks. They say that when you visit Cognac, France, you can actually smell the evaporating cognac in the air. Now, give or take a

Brandy and Cognac Snifters

- Brandy and cognac glasses are called "snifters." A proper serving is 2 ounces.

- Most snifters are short stemmed and big bowled.

- Snifters are available in sizes of 5–26 ounces.

- Most times you can tip a snifter onto its side, then pour brandy to the rim, and that will be a perfect portion.

Brandy

- Brandy can be made with any fruits anywhere in the world.

- The word *brandy* is of Dutch origin and means "burnt wine."

- Brandy dates back to the twelfth century, but

most historians believe it dates back much further. Documented proof has not surfaced.

- Popular fruit brandy flavors are apple, blackberry, pear, peach, and apricot.

bottle or two, normally there is enough cognac being aged at all times (in $4,000 oak casks) to fill over a billion bottles. This means that every year almost 200,000 bottles of cognac disappear into thin air. And the angels aren't sharing.

Maurice Hennessey was the first winemaker to begin a grading system for cognac in 1865. Every cognac bottle is graded, and the grade is put on the label. The cognac grades are V.S. (very superior or three-star; aged a minimum of three years), V.S.O.P. (very superior old pale or reserve; aged four to twenty years), and X.O. (extra old; aged six to forty or more years).

It's interesting how the media can change a spirit's category overnight. For centuries, cognac has been the spirit for the refined. Then around the millennium, rap artists mentioned cognac in their songs, giving cognac a new demographic.

Armagnac

- Armagnac is a high-end brandy made from grapes in the Armagnac region of France.

- Armagnac is the oldest distilled wine in France, dating back to the 1300s.

- It is the only true rival of cognac.

- Only ten varieties of grapes are authorized to be used for Armagnac.

Cognac

- All cognac is brandy, but not all brandy is cognac.

- Cognac is made only from grapes grown in the Cognac region of France.

- Cognac is distilled twice, then aged in oak casks

made from Limousin or Troncais oak wood from trees that grow in the Cognac region.

- The aging process is very expensive because 3 percent of the cognac evaporates.

VODKA

Possibly the first clear spirit to have been invented

In the simplest terms, distillation is the process by which a liquid is boiled and the condensation of the steam is collected. It's believed that ancient alchemists used this process to make medicine and perfumes. No one knows when distillation was first used to make spirits, but we do know the first names it had: "ardent waters" (burnt water), "eau-de-vie" (the water of life), and then "voda" (vodka). Many believe vodka has been around since the 1300s, but it was not like the clean, clear vodka of today. It's believed that makers infused it with herbs, flowers, and fruits.

Smirnoff vodka was the first to use charcoal filtering in 1870. The Smirnoff distillery produced up to four million cases of vodka per year, but in 1917 the Bolsheviks confiscated the distillery after the Russian Revolution. Members of the Smirnov family fled for their lives. One of the Smirnov sons, Vladimir, settled in Paris, changed his last name to "Smirnoff,"

The First Vodka in America

- Piotr Arsenyevitch Smirnov founded his vodka distillery in Moscow in 1860.

- Smirnoff vodka was the first vodka to be introduced to America.

- The Moscow Mule was the first Smirnoff cocktail intro-

duced in1941 by John G. Martin and Jack Morgan.

- Vodka exploded when James Bond ordered a vodka martini, shaken not stirred, in the 1962 film *Dr. No.*

Ultra-premium Vodka

- High-end, boutique, and ultra-premium vodkas hit the market around the millennium.

- Master marketer Sidney Frank is responsible for introducing Grey Goose vodka, the first heavily marketed ultra-premium vodka.

- High-end vodkas focus on sleek and modern bottle design and multiple filtering.

- Ketel One vodka has won many blind vodka taste tests.

then opened a distillery. After American Prohibition ended in 1933, Vladimir sold the American rights to Smirnoff vodka to a friend, Rudolph Kunett, but Kunett's American vodka adventures were unsuccessful. He sold the rights to John G. Martin. Today Smirnoff is owned by drinks giant Diageo and is the top-selling vodka in the world.

ZOOM

More on Vodka
Vodka provides a blank canvas that allows much experimentation. Companies infuse it with flavors, make it from organic materials, color it black, or harvest chunks of icebergs to use as their water. College students have even been known to run cheap vodka through a water filter a few times to make it taste like premium vodka.

Flavored Vodka

- Absolut introduced the first infused/flavored vodka in 1986 called "Absolut Peppar." It's flavored with three types of peppers, making it perfect for a Bloody Mary.

- Almost every vodka brand has a line of flavored vodka.

- Absolut Citron exploded the vodka infusion world with lemon drops and cosmopolitans.

- Second to flavor its vodkas was Stolichnaya.

Absolut Ads

Absolut has always been known for its clever ads. The first Absolut ad was called "Absolut Perfection." It was introduced in 1980. Since then, there have been over fifteen hundred ads. Current marketing techniques range from using flavors to represent cities to covering bottles in red sequins.

SPIRITS

GIN
The clear, historic spirit is distilled with many herbs and botanicals

Gin in its basic form is vodka that has been redistilled with herbs and botanicals. The main categories of gin are Genever, London Dry, Plymouth, and the 2007 addition of New Western Dry. Gin has been known to be made in Holland, England, Germany, France, America, Spain, Lithuania, Belgium, Canada, and Slovakia.

Many people believe that the fifteenth-century Dutch professor and physician Dr. Sylvius invented gin for medicinal purposes. However, others believe that the sixteenth-century Dutch professor and physician Dr. Sylvius invented gin. Yes, historians discovered that two men of the same name and profession were credited with inventing gin. Historians also discovered the first major mention of juniper-based, health-related tonics and medicines in the Dutch publication *Der Naturen Bloeme* by Jacob van Maerlant te Damme in 1269. We also know that Holland is credited with making the first

Genever

- Genever is considered the first gin.

- Genever is made in Holland, two provinces in West Germany, and two in Northern France.

- The modern categories of Genever are *oude, jonge, graajenever,* and *korenwijn.*

- In 2008, by a European declaration "jonge" and "oude" Genever may only be labeled and sold as such in Holland and Belgium.

London Dry

- London Dry gin is believed to have originated with British troops who brought Dutch gin back to England after the Third Dutch War in the late 1600s.

- London Dry gin has a crisp, dry taste that mixes well in cocktails.

- This gin is the most common and widely distributed.

- London Dry gin brands include Beefeater, Bombay, Tanqueray, and Boodles.

commercial gin, called "Genever." Genever's taste is sweet and malty. The word *jonge* means the young and new way of distilling, *oude* means the old and traditional way, and *korenwijn* is as close to the original recipe as possible. The first gin in England was sweet like Dutch gin. The first popular brand was Old Tom gin, and it's the last remaining sweet English gin today. Its name came from a wooden plaque shaped like a black cat (tom cat) that was mounted on the outside wall of a pub. Patrons placed a penny in the cat's mouth, then put their lips around a small tube between the cat's paws. The tavern keeper inside would then pour a shot of Old Tom gin through the tube and into the patron's mouth.

The Plymouth category of gin has one gin— called "Plymouth." The gin is fruity and aromatic. It's made in Plymouth, England, and Plymouth Coates & Co. owns all rights.

New Western Dry

- New Western Dry gin is a category coined by master mixologist Ryan Magarian.

- These gins include Aviation, Hendrick's, and Martin Miller's.

- New Western Dry gins let juniper ride in the backseat, with a focus on the other herbs and botanicals in the front seat. They also seem to have a delicate and fresh hint of cucumber.

Gin Madness

In the 1700s, gin was cheaper than ale, and London turned into a slum full of poverty and despair. This time in history was called "Gin Madness." Artist William Hogarth captured the time when he engraved "Gin Lane" in 1750. The Gin Act was passed in 1736, and the Gin Riots spread to the streets of London. After this time, many people began distilling their own gin.

RUM

Get super sweet on the tropical spirit that is made with sugarcane

Rum can be made from sugarcane or from its by-products: sugarcane juice and molasses. Since the 1600s, rum has been used for trading, drinking, bribing, and even paying wages.

Some believe the Dutch first brought sugarcane to Barbados. Others say that sugarcane was first used in China. What we do know is that brothers Don and Jose Bacardi, Spanish businessmen who immigrated to Cuba, created the first real commercial rum in1862. It took them ten years to perfect the once-crude sugarcane spirit into a smooth, refined spirit. Due to wars and other conflicts, Bacardi rum went through many tribulations. Finally, in the 1930s, the factory moved to San Juan, Puerto Rico, where it is headquartered today.

Gold rums have a richer and silkier flavor and texture than light rums. My favorite is Appleton's from Jamaica. In the 1800s, there were almost 150 rum distilleries in Jamaica, and today there are five. One of them is Appleton's.

Light Rum

- Light rum is also known as "silver," "white," or "platinum rum."

- Light rum doesn't require aging and is usually bottled after distillation.

- Brazil makes a rum from Brazilian sugarcane that they call "cachaça" (pronounced ka-SHAH-sa). The popular cocktail called the "caipirinha" (pronounced kai-pee-REEN-ya) is made with it.

- Bacardi is the most popular light rum worldwide.

Gold Rum

- Gold rum is sometimes called "amber rum."

- The gold color comes from the rum's being aged in wooden barrels.

- Some gold rums make great mixing rums, and others are excellent for sipping like a fine cognac. It mostly depends on aging.

- Some premium gold rums are actually blends rums that have been aged up to ten years.

Dark rum is usually made with molasses in tropical locations all over the world. An affluent, first-born Englishman, James Gosling, created Gosling's Black Seal Rum. In the spring of 1806, Gosling set sail for America on a ship named the *Mercury*. The ship carried £10,000 in merchandise that would be used to open a shop. But sea storms swept him to St. George's port in Bermuda, and he accepted the detour as a sign that this is where he was meant to be. Eighteen years later he sent for his brother, and they began making rum.

Two other rum categories are over proof rum and super premium sipping rum. Over proof rums are used to flame a drink or used for culinary purposes. Super premium sipping rums are also called "añejo rums."

Dark Rum

- Dark rum is also known as "black rum."

- Myers's Original Dark Rum is the most popular dark rum in the world. It's made from 100 percent Jamaican molasses.

- Two dark rums are used in famous recipes: Gosling's Black Seal Rum in a dark 'n stormy and Myers's Dark Rum in a planter's punch.

- Dark rum is often used as a floater on top of a tropical drink.

Flavored Rum

These rums come in a wide variety of flavors.

- Flavors include coconut, banana, mango, raspberry, vanilla, spiced, pineapple, citron, passion fruit, orange, and lime.

- In 1984, Captain Morgan Spiced Rum became the first flavored rum available in America.

- Malibu Coconut Rum was released in the early 1980s as well but classified as a liqueur with rum and coconut flavorings. Today the distillery claims that it's now made with rum.

SPIRITS

TEQUILA
Learn about the national spirit from the country south of the border

Historians say that the Aztecs were making an alcoholic drink from the agave plant as early as the first century; fifteen hundred years later the Spanish invaded Mexico and took the agave-type wine and distilled it. One hundred years later the town of Tequila was allowed to make Mezcal; 150 years later the Spanish crown granted a distillery license to Jose Cuervo. Much happened in the next one hundred years due to Mexico trying to gain its independence from Spain, but by the late 1800s Mexico and tequila became firmly established.

The *numero uno* thing to know about tequila is that by law it can be produced only in the Tequila region of Mexico. The *numero dos* thing to know is that in order for a label to say "tequila" it must be made from at least 51 percent blue agave. If it's not, then it's called a "mixto" (this is a good example of Mezcal).

There are over two hundred types of agave plants, but the

Blanco Tequila

- Blanco is also called "silver" or "white tequila."

- Most times blanco tequila is either bottled straight out of the still or filtered, then bottled.

- If stored, blanco tequila must not be kept longer than sixty days in stainless steel tanks for no aging.

- One hundred percent agave blanco tequila is an excellent choice to use for margaritas.

Reposado Tequila

- Reposado is a blanco that has been aged in white oak casks for two to twelve months. It has a mellow yellow color and taste.

- The gold color of a reposado comes from aging in the wood casks.

- *Reposado* means "rested" (as in "rested in barrels").

- Reposado is the highest-quality tequila that will still taste good in a margarita. It has a balance between bite and smoothness.

best is the blue agave plant. An agave plant takes almost ten years to mature. When it matures a flower stalk grows straight up through the plant. If allowed to grow it will bloom yellow flowers, but if the agave farmer chops off the stalk, the plant will swell inside, creating a large bulb that will fill with a sweet, juicy pulp. This forms into the piña, which is the part of the agave plant that is used to make tequila. The piña (which means "pineapple" because it looks kind of like a pineapple) can weigh as much as one hundred pounds. The piñas are cut, baked, and then crushed to extract the sweet agave juice

used to make tequila. The worm in Mezcal is just a moth larva that grows inside agave plants.

Anejos are typically aged between one and eight years.

Añejo Tequila

- Añejo is a blanco tequila that has been aged for more than one year.

- High-quality añejos are aged up to three years.

- Añejo that is aged up to eight years is called "reserva." There is controversy over letting tequila age this long because the oak begins to overwhelm the agave flavor.

  - *Añejo* means "old."

Gold Tequila

Gold tequila (also called "oro") is a blanco tequila that has had coloring (usually caramel) and/or flavor added to it to make it appear that it's been aged. It's usually a mixto. The best example of this is Jose Cuervo. The term *gold* does not refer to a reposado or an añejo because they are gold in color.

WHISKEY/WHISKY
Amber waves of grain are mashed up, aged, and then poured into a bottle

Today whiskey/whisky is made all over the world in places such as India, Japan, Germany, France, and Russia, but the four most prominent countries that have been making whiskey/whisky for centuries are Scotland, Ireland, America, and Canada. Even today Ireland and Scotland still bicker over who invented whiskey/whisky first. By the way, Irish and American whiskey is spelled with an "e" and Scotland's and Canada's whisky is not.

Blended Irish whiskey makes up the majority of Irish whiskey. Single-malt Irish whiskey is made from one whiskey type in either column or pot stills. Grain Irish whiskey is made from 100 percent Irish grain and is usually used for blends. And pure pot still Irish whiskey is made from a combination of

Irish Whiskey

- Ireland makes blended, single-malt, grain, and pure pot still whiskey.

- There are only three distilleries in the entire country of Ireland.

- Irish whiskey is made from malt that is dried in sealed ovens and usually distilled three times.

- There are two popular Irish whiskey-based liqueurs: Bailey's Original Irish Cream and Irish Mist.

Scotch Whisky

- Scotland makes blended Scotch whisky and single-malt whisky.

- Scotch whisky is known for its smoky flavor, which comes from drying malted barley over open peat fires.

- Scotland is divided into four geographical flavors: Lowlands, Highlands, Speyside, and the Islands.

- A popular Scotch-based liqueur from Scotland is Drambuie. It's made from heather honey and herbs.

malted and unmalted barley, then distilled in pot stills.

A fifteen-year-old boy, Johnnie Walker, is credited with first blending Scotch whisky. In 1820, his father died, and Johnnie used the life insurance money to open a small general store. At the time, tea was all the rave, and he got the idea of blending the single-malt whiskys like the tea in his store was blended. All four whisky-making regions in Scotland produce different-tasting Scotches.

The term *bourbon* comes from Bourbon County (Kentucky) barrels being labeled as such. Bourbon breaks down into two premium bourbon categories: small batch and single barrel. Small-batch bourbons are bottlings from a batch of barrels, and single-barrel bourbons come from a single barrel of bourbon. Corn whiskey is basically moonshine, and rye must be made from at least 51 percent rye. The most popular American blended whiskey is Seagram's 7. Tennessee whiskey is made in Tennessee. The most popular Tennessee whiskeys are Jack Daniel's and George Dickel. You may hear of "sour mash," which means that part of a previous batch is used to start a new batch.

Canadian Whisky

- Canada blends its whisky for a smoother taste.

- Often Canada calls its whisky "rye" but doesn't follow strict laws about how much rye must be in the whisky.

- Crown Royal Canadian whisky was made by Seagram's especially for Queen Elizabeth's visit in 1939.

- Remember, Canada and Scotland spell *whisky* without an e. America and Ireland spell *whiskey* with an e.

American Whiskey

- America produces five kinds of whiskey: bourbon, corn, rye, blended, and Tennessee.

- By federal law bourbon can be made only in America and made with at least 51 percent American corn.

- Only bourbon made in Kentucky can have the words "Kentucky bourbon" on a label.

- In 1964, an act of Congress declared bourbon as "America's Native Spirit" as well as the country's official distilled spirit.

LIQUEURS

Learn the differences between the many liqueurs made around the world

Who knows what liqueurs ancient alchemists created in their dens? We do know that Dark Age and Middle Age monks and physicians experimented with liqueurs to serve medicinal purposes or to find the elixir of life.

By the civilized nineteenth century, liqueurs were drunk as an apéritif (before-dinner drink) or as an after-dinner diges-

tive drink. Italians have been known for a long time to drink Sambuca before dinner and shots of Limoncello after. Other popular Italian liqueurs include Tuaca, Galliano, Frangelico, and DiSaronno Amaretto. Germans are known to drink peppermint schnapps after dinner, but the most popular liqueur from Germany is Jägermeister. Almost every country in the

Liqueurs

- There are over five hundred commercial liqueurs in the world.

- Liqueurs are sweet flavor-infused spirits and can also be called "cordials."

- Liqueurs can be low-proof, high-proof, cream, crème, or schnapps.

- Liqueurs are considered a modifier in the cocktail world. They are used in small quantities to add flavor to a drink.

Cream Liqueurs

- Cream liqueurs are made with dairy cream and a spirit base.

- Baileys Original Irish Cream is the most popular cream liqueur in the world. It was the first cream and paved the way for many others.

- Most cream liqueurs have a shelf life of two years.

- Some bars keep cream liqueurs in the cooler or fridge.

world has at least one liqueur. Popular French liqueurs include Chambord, Cointreau, Chartreuse, St-Germain Elderflower, Grand Marnier, Bénédictine, and the crème family. Spain has Licor 43, Greece has Ouzo, the U.S. has Southern Comfort, Switzerland has Goldschlager, Jamaica has Tia Maria, Mexico has Kahlúa, Japan has Sakura, South Africa has Amarula, and the list goes on and on.

Today many liqueurs are used to enhance the flavor of a recipe. In most cases, the liqueur is always the smaller portion of alcohol (sometimes called a modifier) that goes into a cocktail.

ZOOM

Baileys Original Irish Cream is a combination of cream from Irish cows, Irish whiskey, chocolate, and vanilla. It took the Baileys creators four years of experimenting to find a method to keep the cream from curdling when mixed with Irish whiskey. Finally in 1974 they succeeded.

Crème Liqueurs

- *Crème* is a French word that is pronounced "krem."

- Crèmes have a lot of sugar added to them, which results in a syrupy consistency.

- The most popular crèmes are crème de cacao (light and dark) and crème de menthe (white/clear and green).

- Other crèmes include crème de banana, crème de cassis (black currants), and crème de Yvette (violets).

Schnapps

- The word *schnapps* is of German descent and means "swallow."

- Schnapps is usually a high-proof liqueur because it is made from fermented fruits, grain, or herbs, then distilled.

- True German schnapps does not have added sugar.

- American schnapps tends to be very sweet. This is because sugar is added after distillation.

SPIRITS

AMERICAN WHISKEY COCKTAILS
Master the cocktails that pioneered the way for all others that followed

As far as we know, the cocktail is an American invention, and American whiskey is believed to have been the fuel that lit the trail into the wide-open spaces of cocktail culture history. Because American whiskey has been around since the late 1700s, it's not surprising that cocktail historians have found recipes in print since the early 1800s. The mint julep and the

Sazerac tie for the title of first cocktail, but it didn't take long for every spirit to follow suit.

The Mint Julep is steeped in southern American tradition. The recipe is simple, and sometimes simplicity is best. The Sazerac is a perfect example of a balanced cocktail using five distinct flavors, and yet when it is sipped like a proper cocktail

Sazerac

Ingredients

¼ ounce absinthe
2 ounces rye whiskey
½ ounce simple syrup
½ ounce filtered water
3 dashes Peychaud's bitters
Ice
Lemon twist for garnish

1. Chill a 4–6-ounce rocks glass, then swirl with absinthe.
2. Pour all ingredients except the absinthe into a mixing glass filled half with ice and stir.
3. Strain into the chilled cocktail glass. Twist garnish but do not drop in.

Mint Julep

Ingredients

Fingertip full of spearmint leaves (one sprig for garnish)
1 teaspoon sugar
Ice
2 ounces bourbon whiskey
1 ounce simple syrup

1. Muddle mint and sugar in a mint julep cup.
2. Fill the cup with crushed ice.
3. Pour in the bourbon and simple syrup and stir until the julep cup is frosty.
4. Add more crushed ice. Add garnish.

should be sipped, one can taste and smell each flavor.

It's not unusual that the Ward Eight and Manhattan, two American whiskey cocktails from the late 1800s, were conceived during political events because only politicians, men of importance, and men of affluence patronized the elegant cocktail bars serving these cocktails. Working-class men mostly drank beer, wine, and whiskey shots at local watering holes. And women, well, women were not allowed to patronize any bar at any time unless they were working girls.

Manhattan

Ingredients

Ice
2 ounces rye or bourbon whiskey
1 ounce sweet vermouth
2 dashes Angostura bitters
Maraschino cherry garnish

1. Chill a 4–6-ounce cocktail glass.
2. Fill a mixing glass half with ice.
3. Pour in the ingredients and stir with ice.
4. Strain into the chilled cocktail glass. Add garnish.

Manhattan by Train

The birth of the Manhattan is believed to have occurred in the 1880s. In the 1900s, the cocktail graced many films and TV shows. One of the most memorable was the 1959 comedy, *Some Like It Hot*, starring Marilyn Monroe and Jack Lemmon. Marilyn's character, Sugar, makes a batch of Manhattans on a train by pouring smuggled ingredients into a hot water bottle.

SCOTCH WHISKY COCKTAILS
Scotland cashes in on the new cocktail culture action

Scotland to this day—and every day forward—takes the credit for having made the first whisky. The Scots will even show you their documented proof from the late 1400s. So, it's not any surprise that they would trek to America via stagecoach and a two-month passenger ship voyage across the Atlantic to make their mark into the cocktail world. And that's just what Tommy Dewar, the charming, charismatic son of John Dewar Sr. of Dewar's White Label blended Scotch whisky

set out to do. His efforts proved successful when he became part of the world's first film commercial, which projected his Scotch whisky onto a wall overlooking Herald Square in New York City in 1898. It's believed that shortly after this event, the cocktail called the "Rob Roy" was created.

The Rob Roy was named after a Scottish folk hero often referred to in Scotland as the "Scottish Robin Hood." In the cocktail world, the Rob Roy often was referred to as "the cousin

Rob Roy

Ingredients

Ice
2 ounces blended Scotch whisky
1 ounce sweet vermouth
2 dashes Angostura bitters
Lemon twist garnish

1. Chill a 4–6-ounce cocktail glass.
2. Fill a mixing glass half with ice.
3. Pour in the ingredients and stir with ice.
4. Strain into the chilled cocktail glass. Add garnish.

Rusty Nail

Ingredients

Ice
2 ounces blended Scotch whisky
1 ounce Drambuie
Optional lemon twist garnish

1. Fill a rocks glass with ice.
2. Pour in the ingredients and stir. Add garnish if desired.
3. If preferred sweeter, then simply pour equals parts of blended Scotch whisky and Drambuie.

of the Manhattan." Due to the smoky flavor of Scotch whisky, there weren't as many vintage Scotch-based cocktails created as there were American whiskey cocktails, but there were still enough to suffice.

Drambuie is a Scotch whisky-based heather honey liqueur whose recipe was a gift from Prince Charles Edward (Bonnie Prince Charlie) to Captain John MacKinnon and his family for hiding and protecting him while in Scotland in 1745. Years later it became a popular local liqueur, but it still took another hundred years of MacKinnon generations to begin to market the liqueur commercially worldwide.

Blood and Sand

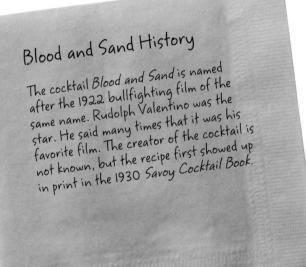

Ingredients

Ice
1 ounce blended Scotch whisky
½ ounce Peter Heering Cherry Heering
½ ounce sweet vermouth
1 ounce fresh blood orange juice
Lime garnish

1. Chill a 7-ounce cocktail glass with ice.
2. Shake ingredients with ice.
3. Strain into the chilled cocktail glass. Add garnish.

Blood and Sand History

The cocktail *Blood and Sand* is named after the 1922 bullfighting film of the same name. Rudolph Valentino was the star. He said many times that it was his favorite film. The creator of the cocktail is not known, but the recipe first showed up in print in the 1930 *Savoy Cocktail Book*.

BRANDY COCKTAILS
Brandy was considered dandy for many cocktails far and wide

It might surprise you to learn that the Brandy Alexander was probably the first popular chocolate martini in cocktail history. It was supposedly created for the 1922 arranged royal wedding of Lord Viscount Lascelles and Princess Mary at Westminster Abbey in London. She was twenty-four, and he was forty. Nonetheless, this sweet, chocolate brandy cocktail garnished with nutmeg was perfect for a winter wedding and became popular thereafter. It even made it to the first

episode of the *Mary Tyler Moore* TV show and also is believed to have been John Lennon's favorite cocktail.

Royalty scores another point because it's strongly believed that Sidecars were served at the spring 1956 wedding of Grace Kelly and Prince Rainier III at the palace of Monaco.

To hip you up on vintage cocktail lingo, a Crusta is a cocktail served in a chilled wine glass with a whole rind of citrus inside. The Brandy Crusta is the granddaddy on this page of

Brandy Alexander

Ingredients

Ice
1½ ounces brandy
1½ ounces dark crème de cocoa
2 ounces cream
Sprinkle of nutmeg for garnish

1. Chill a 7-ounce cocktail glass with ice.
2. Shake ingredients with ice.
3. Strain into the chilled cocktail glass. Add garnish.
4. Can be made over ice or blended with vanilla ice cream.

Sidecar

Ingredients

Sugar to rim glass
1 ounce brandy
1 ounce Cointreau
1 ounce fresh lemon juice
Ice

1. Chill a 7-ounce cocktail glass, then rim with sugar.
2. Shake ingredients with ice.
3. Strain into the cocktail glass.

vintage brandy cocktails because it's been around since the 1850s. Joe Santini in New Orleans created it.

The Stinger is a popular and sweet cocktail that really packs a punch. Frank Sinatra, Katharine Hepburn, Grace Kelly, and Bette Midler have drunk it on the silver screen.

ZOOM

Croatian monks on the peninsula of Zadar are known for first making a liqueur using marasca cherries in the 1500s. One hundred years later it was named "Maraschino liqueur." It spread to every European port and led England's King George IV and Queen Victoria to order shiploads. Others who admired the liqueur were Napoleon Bonaparte, Russian Czar Nicholas I, and French King Louis XVIII.

Brandy Crusta

Ingredients

Sugar to rim glass
2 ounces brandy
½ ounce Maraschino liqueur
¾ ounce orange Curacao
½ ounce fresh lemon juice
1 dash Angostura bitters
Whole lemon peel garnish

1. Chill a wine glass, then rim heavily with sugar.
2. Shake ingredients with ice.
3. Strain into the wine glass. Add garnish.

Stinger

Ingredients

Ice
1 ounce brandy
½ ounce white crème de menthe

1. Fill a rocks glass with ice.
2. Pour in the ingredients and stir.
3. If preferred sweeter, then simply pour equals parts of brandy and white crème de menthe.

GIN COCKTAILS
Gin was "in" for the golden age of vintage to post-Prohibition cocktails

Believe it or not, America's first distillery was built in the 1640s on Staten Island, and it produced gin. It's hard to believe that it took another two hundred years for the cocktail to be in vogue. With the exception of the Gin Martini (found in Chapter 7 on martinis), these four cocktails represent true vintage gin cocktails of days gone by.

Henry C. Ramos invented the Ramos Gin Fizz in 1888 in New Orleans. My guess is that most New Orleans bartenders cursed his name—under their breath, of course—for the next thirty-three years. My point being that to make the drink took time and effort; liken it to the revived Mojito craze of the millennium. The secret ingredients remained . . . well, secret until Prohibi-

Ramos Gin Fizz

Nineteen-fourteen

Ingredients

2 ounces gin
½ ounce fresh lemon juice
½ ounce fresh lime juice
2 ounces cream
1 teaspoon sugar
1 organic egg white
3 drops orange flower water
Ice
2 ounces charged soda water

1. Chill a tall glass.
2. Shake ingredients (except soda water) with ice for one minute.
3. Strain into the wine glass.
4. Add soda water.

Ingredients

Ice
2 ounces gin
½ ounce Cointreau
½ ounce fresh lemon juice
Half an organic egg white

1. Chill a 7-ounce cocktail glass with ice.
2. Shake ingredients with ice.
3. Strain into the chilled cocktail glass.
4. If preferred sweeter, then add more Cointreau.

tion in 1921: lime and lemon juice, orange flower water, real cream, egg white, and, oh yes, gin. Bartenders had to shake the drink up to two minutes for the proper chill and blending of the ingredients. The governor would even take a NOLA bartender with him on trips to the White House so he could have fresh Ramos Gin Fizzes. As for the obscure ingredient, orange flower water, don't attempt to substitute for it because doing so won't work. This water is made from the flower petals of Seville orange trees in the Mediterranean region. Today you can purchase it at gourmet and Middle Eastern grocery stores.

The Pegu Club was named after the Rangoon, Burma (Myanmar), gentlemen's club of the same name. Traveling British business gentlemen inspired elite private clubs such as this one so they could have the luxuries of home. The original club no longer stands, but New York City built a Pegu Club in its honor. Inside you can order this cocktail as well as many other vintage cocktails, no matter what your sex.

Pegu Club

Ingredients

Ice
1 ounce gin
1 ounce orange Curaçao
¼ ounce fresh lime juice
1 dash each of orange and Angostura bitters
Lime wedge garnish

1. Chill a 7-ounce cocktail glass with ice.
2. Shake ingredients with ice.
3. Strain into the chilled cocktail glass. Add garnish.

Gimlet

Ingredients

Ice
2 ounces gin
1 ounce Rose's Lime Juice
Lime garnish

1. Chill a 7-ounce cocktail glass with ice.
2. Shake ingredients with ice.
3. Strain into the chilled cocktail glass. Add garnish.
4. Can be made on the rocks as well.

WINE & LIQUEUR COCKTAILS
Sweet, bitter, strong, and weak play a part in these cocktails

The Absinthe Drip is the best example of "what was old is new again." It was illegal in America from 1912 to 2007. Why? The nutshell version is that it was drunk in the early to mid-1800s by high society during the Belle Époque (Beautiful Era) in France. In 1863, France imported American grapes in hopes of cross-breeding and creating a new grape/wine, but the grapevines contained a disease called "phylloxera" and destroyed all of France's crops (as well as most of Europe's).

The price of wine skyrocketed, and absinthe became available for everyone. Many artists, such as Picasso, Van Gogh, and Manet, drank and painted absinthe.

After the wine crops were disease free, members of the wine industry put together a fierce marketing plan to demonize absinthe so that they could win back their wine consumers. They spread gossip and lies about absinthe worldwide through posters and newspapers, which we later

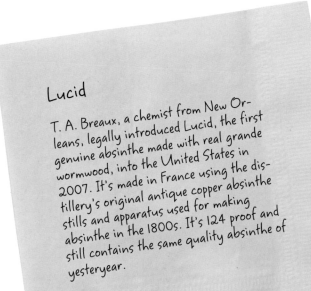

Lucid

T. A. Breaux, a chemist from New Orleans, legally introduced Lucid, the first genuine absinthe made with real grande wormwood, into the United States in 2007. It's made in France using the distillery's original antique copper absinthe stills and apparatus used for making absinthe in the 1800s. It's 124 proof and still contains the same quality absinthe of yesteryear.

Absinthe Drip

Ingredients

1½ ounces absinthe
Sugar cube
½ ounce iced cold water

1. Pour absinthe into the glass.
2. Set an absinthe spoon with a sugar cube on top of the glass.
3. Slowly drip iced cold water over the sugar cube. The cube will melt into the glass.
4. Stir.

disproved. The masses believed the lies, and in 1912 absinthe was banned in every country in the world except for two.

While the French were enjoying their absinthe, one of the cocktails the Italians were drinking was called a "Milano-Torino." Visiting Americans took a liking to it, so it was renamed "Americano." The cocktail was first served in Cafe Campari in Milan in the 1860s.

Americano

Ingredients

Ice
1 ounce sweet vermouth
1 ounce Campari
1 ounce soda water
Lemon twist garnish

1. Chill a 7-ounce cocktail glass with ice.
2. Stir ingredients with ice.
3. Strain into the chilled cocktail glass. Add garnish.
4. Can be made on the rocks as well. Some like to add more soda water.

Sherry Cobbler

Ingredients

Ice
1 tablespoon sugar
5 ounces sherry
Seasonal fruit garnish

1. Fill a tall glass with ice.
2. Add sugar.
3. Pour in sherry and stir.
4. Garnish with fresh seasonal fruit and berries.

RUM COCKTAILS

Island-inspired rum cocktails prove that what was old is new again

Did you think that the Mojito was a new cocktail creation? Yes, it's true that James Bond ordered one with Halle Berry in 2002, but this minty fresh cocktail has been around a long time. In fact, many believe that it derived from African slaves working the fields in Cuba in the 1800s. What we know for sure is that the mojito is mentioned in the Key West, Florida, *Sloppy Joe's Bar Manual* from the early 1930s. America was in the Prohibition era until 1933, so the affluent would make

their way down to Havana and party. One place in particular was La Bodeguita del Medio. This is where famous writers, artists, musicians, and soon-to-be famous starlets gravitated. And they all drank Mojitos. The bar is still there.

The term *Cuba Libre* means "free Cuba," and that's the cry that was heard throughout the Battle of Santiago de Cuba (Spanish-American War) in 1898. It's believed that the drink Cuba Libre was created around that time. Legend has it that

Mojito

Ingredients

Fingertip full of mint leaves
½ a lime, cut
Ice
1½ ounces Cuban light rum
1 ounce simple syrup
4 ounces soda water
Sprig of mint garnish

1. Muddle the mint and limes in a double old-fashioned glass.
2. Fill with crushed or cracked ice.
3. Pour in the rum, simple syrup, and soda water.
4. Stir and add garnish.

Cuba Libre

Ingredients

Ice
2 lime wedges for garnish
6 ounces cola
2 ounces light rum

1. Fill a tall or highball glass with ice.
2. Squeeze one juicy lime wedge over the ice and discard.
3. Add the cola and rum.
4. Squeeze the second lime and drop in the drink. Stir.

Teddy Roosevelt and his Rough Riders were drinking Cuba Libres and brought the drink back to New York. The drink had another resurrection during World War II when the Andrews Sisters' hit song, "Rum & Coca-Cola," was heard on radios everywhere.

Milk Punch

Ingredients

Ice
2 ounces light rum
1 ounce simple syrup
4 ounces whole milk
Nutmeg and cinammon for garnish

1. Fill a 12-ounce glass with ice.
2. Add ingredients and stir.
3. Garnish with nutmeg and cinnamon.
4. For more flavor, you can substitute the light rum for dark rum.

Guys and Dolls

In the 1955 film, Guys and Dolls, Marlon Brando takes church lady Jean Simmons to Cuba on a date. At dinner, he orders Milk Punches. Jean asks about the flavoring in the Milk Punch, and he tells her that at night they put a preservative called "Bacardi" in the milk. She drinks several of them.

CLASSIC MARTINIS
Master these for a solid martini-making foundation

The martini is without doubt the king of cocktails. It's an icon in modern society as well as in the cocktail culture worldwide. Since the mid-1800s, the Classic Martini has risen and fallen in popularity and has gone through many ingredient changes, but the common denominator has always been gin. Some say making a martini is simple, whereas others believe it's an artform. A Classic Martini should always be stirred and never shaken because shaking a cocktail adds air, resulting in

a light and bubbly feel on the tongue. In addition, it dilutes much water into the cocktail. Stirring a martini keeps the alcohol smooth and silky, yielding a perfect portion of dilution from the ice. To reach a chilled temperature, stir twenty times clockwise, then twenty times counterclockwise.

You should always prechill a cocktail glass when making a Classic Martini. The martini is all about being very cold. You can have glasses ready from the freezer or prechill by put-

Classic Martini

Ingredients

Ice
2 ounces gin
¼ ounce dry vermouth
2 large olives and/or a lemon twist garnish

1. Chill a 4–6-ounce cocktail glass.
2. Fill a mixing glass half with ice.
3. Pour in the ingredients and stir with ice.
4. Strain into the chilled cocktail glass. Add garnish.

Gibson

Ingredients

Ice
2 ounces gin
¼ ounce dry vermouth
Garnish with 2 cocktail onions

1. Chill a 4–6-ounce cocktail glass.
2. Fill a mixing glass half with ice.
3. Pour in the ingredients and stir with ice.
4. Strain into the chilled cocktail glass. Add garnish.

ting ice and water into a glass while making the cocktail. It's also recommended to use smaller vintage-sized glasses (4–6 ounces) to keep the martini cold longer. There's nothing more undesirable than a warm martini halfway down the glass.

Dirty Martini

Ingredients

Ice
2 ounces gin
¼ ounce dry vermouth
½ ounce olive brine
2 large olives and/or a lemon twist garnish

1. Chill a 4–6-ounce cocktail glass.
2. Fill a mixing glass half with ice.
3. Pour in the ingredients and stir with ice.
4. Strain into the chilled cocktail glass. Add garnish.

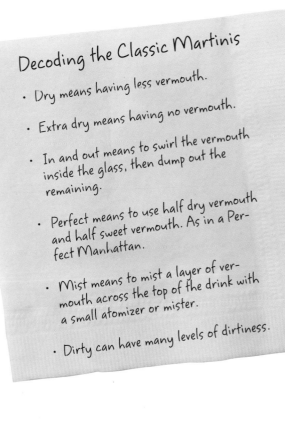

Decoding the Classic Martinis

- Dry means having less vermouth.

- Extra dry means having no vermouth.

- In and out means to swirl the vermouth inside the glass, then dump out the remaining.

- Perfect means to use half dry vermouth and half sweet vermouth. As in a Perfect Manhattan.

- Mist means to mist a layer of vermouth across the top of the drink with a small atomizer or mister.

- Dirty can have many levels of dirtiness.

THE FIRST VODKA MARTINIS
These classics shook things up for every vodka-based martini that followed

In 1953, Ian Fleming wrote the first known Vodka Martini into literature. Not only that, but also it was shaken, not stirred. The novel is *Casino Royale*, the chapter is seven, and the handsome spy who ordered it is James Bond. Bond named the martini after his love interest, Vesper. In 1962, the first James Bond film, *Dr. No*, hit the silver screen showing Bond ordering and shaking a Vodka Martini made with Smirnoff vodka. The interesting fact is that vodka was a new spirit to Americans in the 1950s, and they didn't take a liking to it until the debonair James Bond endorsed it. Today it is the number one spirit nationwide.

The birth of the Cosmopolitan took place in Miami in 1988 when Absolut released its second flavored vodka, Citron.

Vesper

Ingredients

Ice
2 ounces gin
1 ounce vodka
½ ounce Lillet blanc
Lemon twist garnish

1. Chill a 4–6-ounce cocktail glass.
2. Fill a mixing glass half with ice.
3. Pour in the ingredients and stir with ice.
4. Strain into the chilled cocktail glass. Add garnish.

Vodka Martini

Ingredients

Ice
2 ounces vodka
½ ounce dry vermouth
2 large olives and/or a lemon twist garnish

1. Chill a 4–6-ounce cocktail glass.
2. Fill a mixing glass half with ice.
3. Pour in the ingredients and stir with ice.
4. Strain into the chilled cocktail glass. Add garnish.

However, like most things, it took ten years for the scarlet li-bation served in a cocktail glass to spread to the masses. In the mid-1990s, it was available at posh bars and lounges in the shiny cities, but the brightest lights shone in 1999 during the second season of a little TV show entitled *Sex in the City*. From there, what is now nicknamed the "Cosmo" ignited worldwide, opening the floodgates for the vodka-based martinis of today.

ZOOM

James Bond's exact words in Ian Fleming's novel when ordering a martini are, "Three measures of Gordon's, one of vodka, half a measure of Kina Lil-let, shake it very well until it's ice cold, then add a large thin slice of lemon peel. Got it?" The Kina Lillet is extinct, so Lillet Blanc is acceptable in its place.

Original Cosmopolitan

Ingredients

Ice
2 ounces Absolut Citron vodka
½ ounce triple sec
½ ounce lime cordial
1 ounce cranberry juice
Lime wedge garnish

1. Chill a 7–ounce cocktail glass with ice.
2. Shake ingredients with ice.
3. Strain into the chilled cock-tail glass. Add garnish.

Cosmopolitan

Ingredients

Ice
2 ounces citrus vodka
½ ounce Cointreau
½ ounce fresh lime juice
1 ounce cranberry juice
Lemon twist garnish

1. Chill a 7–ounce cocktail glass with ice.
2. Shake ingredients with ice.
3. Strain into the chilled cock-tail glass. Add garnish.

LEMON DROP MARTINIS

Your troubles will melt like lemon drops when you master these treats

Lemon Drop shots and shooters began surfacing at the beginning of the 1990s. The Lemon Drop Martini followed the Cosmopolitan as another citrusy girly drink to be shaken, then strained in a seductively sexy cocktail. The sweet twist is that the rim was frosted with sugar, turning the lemon drop martini into grownup lemonade. The combination of

the sour following the sweet on the tongue is a delectable taste, so it's no surprise that this martini spread pretty fast. However, it was shot into orbit after Rachael Ray and Oprah Winfrey prepared it together on Oprah's TV show in 2006.

To make the best Lemon Drop Martini, you must use fresh squeezed lemon juice and simple syrup, not store-bought

Lemon Drop Martini

Ingredients

Sugar to rim glass
Ice
2 ounces citrus vodka
½ ounce Cointreau
1 ounce fresh lemon juice
1 ounce simple syrup
Lemon wedge/wheel garnish

1. Rim a chilled cocktail glass with sugar.
2. Shake the ingredients with ice.
3. Strain into the chilled sugar rimmed glass. Add garnish.

Raspberry Lemon Drop Martini

Ingredients

Sugar to rim glass
Ice
1 ounce citrus vodka
1 ounce raspberry vodka
½ ounce Chambord
1 ounce fresh lemon juice
1 ounce simple syrup
Lemon wedge/wheel garnish

1. Rim a chilled cocktail glass with sugar.
2. Shake the ingredients with ice.
3. Strain into the chilled sugar-rimmed glass. Add garnish.

sweet-and-sour mix. You can purchase simple syrup, but it's better to make your own. Every lemon yields different amounts of juice, so always squeeze with a hand juicer or other juicer, then measure out the portion you need. You'll get the most juice from a heavy room-temperature lemon. Simply roll the lemon with your palm on the countertop to break up the juice inside, cut in half, then squeeze. Strain through a sieve or mesh strainer to remove the seeds and pulp.

Blueberry Lemon Drop Martini

Ingredients

Blue-colored sugar to rim glass
Ice
1 ounce citrus vodka
1 ounce blueberry vodka
½ ounce Cointreau
1 ounce fresh lemon juice
1 ounce simple syrup
Lemon wheel and 3 blueberries for garnish

1. Rim a chilled cocktail glass with sugar.
2. Shake the ingredients with ice.
3. Strain into the chilled blue sugar-rimmed glass. Add garnish.

Banana Drop Martini

Ingredients

Yellow-colored sugar to rim glass
Ice
1 ounce citrus vodka
1 ounce banana vodka
½ ounce Cointreau
1 ounce fresh lemon juice
1 ounce simple syrup
Lemon wheel garnish

1. Rim a chilled cocktail glass with sugar.
2. Shake the ingredients with ice.
3. Strain into the chilled yellow sugar-rimmed glass. Add garnish.

CHOCOLATE MARTINIS
Make these decadent drinks to be the envy of all your friends

The basics of a Chocolate-tini are simple: vodka and chocolate liqueur shaken with ice, then strained into a chilled cocktail glass. The beautiful thing is that chocolate goes well with so many other flavors, so you can introduce a myriad of ingredients into a chocolate martini. Chocolate complements orange, lemon, mint, banana, strawberry, raspberry, cream, vanilla, nuts, butterscotch, pepper, cinnamon, whiskey, Champagne, cherry, clove, coconut, coffee, and pear. All

of these possibilities make the shaking field wide open.

You can see that by incorporating different-flavored liquors, liqueurs, and mixers, chocolate martinis are limited only by your imagination. The three base vodkas to use in a Chocolate-tini are a two-ounce portion of plain, vanilla, or chocolate vodka. If you add another flavored vodka in addition to a base vodka, then you would reduce the portion size to one ounce. Flavored vodka choices could be raspberry, strawberry, banana, cherry,

Chocolate-tini

Ingredients

Shredded dark chocolate rim for garnish
Ice
2 ounces vodka
2 ounces white crème de cacao

1. Shred chocolate with a vegetable peeler.
2. Rim a chilled cocktail glass with shredded chocolate.
3. Shake the ingredients with ice.
4. Strain into the chilled chocolate-rimmed glass.

White Chocolate-tini

Ingredients

Chocolate syrup garnish
Ice
1 ounce vanilla vodka
½ ounce white crème de cacao
½ ounce Godiva white chocolate liqueur
1 ounce half-and-half

1. Rim a chilled cocktail glass with chocolate syrup.
2. Shake the ingredients with ice.
3. Strain into the chocolate syrup-rimmed glass.

coconut, lemon, and orange. Liqueur choices are plentiful. Taking a trip to your local liquor store's liqueur section will spawn a world of possibilities. Simply pick out flavors you like but also know that there will be a range of prices and choices for every flavor.

Chocolate begins as a bean picked from the tropical cacao (pronounced ka-COW) tree. After being fermented, roasted, then ground, it's mixed with other ingredients such as sugar, lecithin, and cocoa butter to create powder, alcohol, candy, lotion, and more. This makes possible the fun part of dressing up and garnishing a chocolate martini. You can rim a glass with cocoa powder, powdered hot chocolate mix, shredded chocolate, and so forth. The inside of the glass can be coated in chocolate syrups, and the garnishes can range from the many choices of chocolate candy available, bite-sized chocolate cakes, brownies, cookies, and more!

Strawberry Chocolate-tini

Ingredients

Chocolate and strawberry syrup and a chocolate-dipped strawberry garnish
Ice
1 ounce vanilla vodka
1 ounce strawberry vodka
1 ounce white crème de cacao
1 ounce half and half

1. Crisscross the syrups into a cocktail glass.
2. Shake the ingredients with ice.
3. Strain into the chocolate and strawberry syrup cocktail glass.

Syrup Techniques

Transfer the syrup from the clunky, plastic, store-bought bottles into some condiment squirt bottles, such as those used at picnics for ketchup or mustard. The mouth will be much smaller, allowing you lots of control to make any design. When making many drinks for a party, set the glasses on wax paper and swirl or crisscross your heart out.

APPLETINIS

Sweet-and-sour liquid goodness may be just what the doctor ordered

If Eve had owned a cocktail shaker, then these martinis are what she would have served to Adam. Most definitely the number one ingredient you'll need for an Appletini is apple schnapps—sour apple schnapps, that is. Just know that there are many generic brands of sour apple schnapps. The most flavorful one is neon green and has the word *pucker* in it. It

will taste exactly like a green apple Jolly Rancher.

The Appletini hit the trendy wet spots of the world immediately after the Lemon Drop Martini because it was then that sour apple schnapps was introduced. It was an overnight sensation.

Garnishes for the Appletini family are mostly simple, and

Appletini

Ingredients

Ice
1 ounce citrus vodka
1 ounce sour apple schnapps
1 ounce fresh lemon juice
1 ounce simple syrup
Cherry or Granny Smith apple slice garnish

1. Chill a 7-ounce cocktail glass with ice.
2. Shake ingredients with ice.
3. Strain into the chilled cocktail glass. Add garnish.

Washington Appletini

Ingredients

Ice
1 ounce whiskey
1 ounce sour apple schnapps
2 ounces cranberry juice

1. Chill a 7-ounce cocktail glass with ice.
2. Shake ingredients with ice.
3. Strain into the chilled cocktail glass.

some Appletinis are not garnished at all. This fact does not limit you; in fact, you are free to apply your imagination. Ideas could include sticking a piece of caramel on the rim of a Caramel Appletini or swirling caramel inside the glass of a Caramel Appletini. A Washington Appletini could be garnished with a red Washington apple slice, and any Appletini could be garnished with a Granny Smith apple slice. And on the wild side, you could drop green apple-flavored candy into them like jelly beans or hard candy.

ZOOM

Jolly Rancher candy got its name from the Golden, Colorado, company owners, Bill and Dorothy Harmsen. They felt that the name has a friendly, western sound. Today Hershey owns the candy. For fun you can make your own green apple-flavored vodka. Drop ten green apple Jolly Ranchers into your favorite vodka overnight. And it'll be ready the next morning.

Caramel Appletini

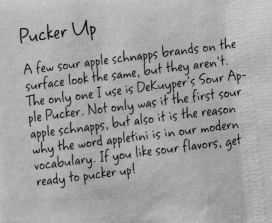

Ingredients

Caramel Syrup
Ice
1 ounce apple vodka
1 ounce sour apple schnapps
1 ounce butterscotch schnapps
1 ounce fresh lemon juice
1 ounce simple syrup
Green apple slice garnish

1. Swirl caramel into a cocktail glass.
2. Shake ingredients with ice.
3. Strain into the cocktail glass. Add garnish.

Pucker Up

A few sour apple schnapps brands on the surface look the same, but they aren't. The only one I use is DeKuyper's Sour Apple Pucker. Not only was it the first sour apple schnapps, but also it is the reason why the word appletini is in our modern vocabulary. If you like sour flavors, get ready to pucker up!

DESSERT MARTINIS
With imagination, you can turn any dessert into a delicious libation

Do you have a favorite dessert, candy, or sweet indulgence? Simply match up the flavors and make a martini. The sky's the limit! Almost every flavor imaginable is represented in a spirit store. Don't limit yourself to flavored spirits; make sure you look at the many flavors available in the liqueur and mixer aisle as well. Need inspiration? Walk down your local grocery store's candy and cake aisle. To determine what portions to match up to a candy bar, for example, simply look at the in-

gredients on the package. The ingredients are always listed from the largest portion to the least.

Cream liqueurs and cream-based mixers are excellent to use for cake batter- or nougat-type dessert martinis. Chocolate liqueurs, of course, are perfect to pour for anything that needs chocolate. If you need a nutty flavor, then try hazelnut liqueur or Amaretto.

Garnishing a dessert martini can be fun. If it's a spinoff of a

Pineapple Upside-down Cake

Almond Joy-tini

Ingredients

1 ounce vanilla vodka
1 ounce Irish cream
2 ounces pineapple juice
Ice
½ ounce grenadine
Pineapple ring, whipped cream, and a cherry garnish

1. Shake the ingredients except for the grenadine and pinapple ring.
2. Shake ingredients with ice.
3. Strain into the chilled cocktail glass.
4. Pour in the grenadine, and it will sink to the bottom. Add garnish.

Ingredients

Chocolate syrup and shredded coconut garnish
Ice
1 ounce vanilla vodka
1 ounce crème de cacao
1 ounce coconut rum
1 ounce half-and-half

1. Rim a cocktail glass with chocolate syrup and coconut flakes.
2. Shake ingredients with ice.
3. Strain into the chilled cocktail glass.

cake or pie, then take inspiration from how these desserts are normally garnished. Add special touches with creative rims made of crushed Oreo cookies, other cookies, sprinkles, and more! While walking the candy, cake, and spice aisles you'll begin to notice all the possibilities.

MAKE IT EASY

You can easily make many nonalcoholic dessert martini versions using flavored extracts from the spice section of your local grocer. There is also an incredible choice of syrup flavors. You'll find an assortment of exotic and unique flavors such as kiwi, huckleberry, pumpkin, tiramisu, and lemongrass. Sugar-free varieties are available, too!

Key Lime Pie-tini

Ingredients

Graham cracker crumbs to rim glass
Ice
2 ounces lime vodka
1 ounce simple syrup
½ ounce lime cordial
1 ounce half-and-half
Whipped cream and lime garnish

1. Rim a cocktail glass with graham cracker crumbs.
2. Shake ingredients with ice.
3. Strain into the chilled cocktail glass. Add garnish.

Key to Stability

Have you ever squirted whipped cream into a drink, and it flopped over? That's because the liquid doesn't provide stability. The trick is to anchor the whipped cream to the side of the glass. You'll find this tip especially helpful for hot drinks because the heat adds to the melting process. The Pineapple Upside-down Cake's stability comes from the pineapple.

THE TYPES OF MARGARITAS

Learn the four main ways to make Mexico's national drink

With many things in life, simpler is better. And this holds true for the margarita. As a matter of fact, the Margarita is the most popular cocktail in the world. A true Margarita is simply tequila, orange liqueur, and fresh lime juice shaken and then strained into a cocktail glass. That's it. Using these three ingredients at a ratio of 3:2:1 is ideal.

The orange liqueur should be all the sweetness a true margarita needs, but a laidback singer named Jimmy Buffett had a hit song in the 1970s entitled "Margaritaville" that caused sweet fake lime margarita premixes to be marketed to meet consumer demand. In the mixer aisle today, you have choices consisting of sour mix, sweet-and-sour mix, limeade, and margarita mix, but the very best mix is homemade. Learn to make it in Chapter 19 (Techniques & Recipes).

As for orange liqueur, you can use triple sec or Curacao. Triple sec is an orange liqueur that has been distilled three

KNACK BARTENDING BASICS

Original Margarita

Ingredients

Ice
2 ounces 100 percent agave blanco tequila
1½ ounces triple sec
1 ounce fresh lime juice

1. Chill a 4–6-ounce cocktail glass with ice.
2. Shake ingredients with ice.
3. Strain into the chilled cocktail glass.
4. You can replace the triple sec with Cointreau.

Classic Margarita

Ingredients

Salt to rim glass (optional)
Ice
2 ounces 100 percent agave tequila of choice
1 ounce triple sec
1 ounce fresh lime juice
1 ounce simple syrup
Lime garnish

1. Chill a 7-ounce cocktail glass with ice.
2. Shake ingredients with ice.
3. Strain into the chilled cocktail glass. Add garnish.
4. You can replace the triple sec with Cointreau.

times (triple), and the word sec is French for "dry." A high-end French triple sec is Cointreau (pronounced QWAN-twoh). Curaçao (pronounced cure-uh-SOW, rhymes with now) is made on the Caribbean island of the same name and comes in three colors: orange, blue, and green.

ZOOM

Cocktail researchers say that a salted rim was never part of the Original Margarita recipe and probably was used later to mask the taste of cheap tequila being added to the drink. Rimming half the glass can please all preferences. At the grocery store, look for choices labeled "coarse sea salt," "margarita salt," or "kosher salt," not table salt.

MARGARITAS

Margarita on the Rocks

Ingredients

Salt to rim glass (optional)
Ice
2 ounces 100 percent tequila of choice
1 ounce triple sec
1 ounce fresh lime juice
1 ounce simple syrup
Lime garnish

1. Rim a margarita glass with salt if desired.
2. Fill the margarita glass with ice.
3. Shake ingredients with ice.
4. Strain into the glass. Add garnish.
5. Shake the ingredients with ice, then strain into salted margarita glass of ice.

Frozen Margarita

Ingredients

Salt to rim glass (optional)
Ice
2 ounces tequila of choice
1 ounce triple sec
1 ounce fresh lime juice
1 ounce simple syrup
Lime garnish

1. Rim a margarita glass with salt if desired.
2. Blend ingredients with a half cup of ice. Add additional ice if needed.
3. Pour into margarita glass. Add garnish.
4. You can replace the triple sec with Cointreau.

PREMIUM MARGARITAS
Raise the bar with some high-end margaritas to really taste the difference

Everything in life has levels from low to high, and the margarita is no exception. By bumping up the quality of tequila and orange liqueur, you'll create a taste with depth and character. The first thing to look for on the tequila label is "100 percent blue agave." The label may read just "100 percent agave." Next, you want it to be either a blanco or a reposado. The blanco

also uses the marketing terms "silver" or "white." An añejo will be more expensive because it is aged longer and filtered more times, but it will have too smooth of a taste, causing it to blend instead of balance the acid of the lime. The blanco or reposado will provide the bite to balance the flavors. Save the añejo for sipping.

Gold Margarita

Ingredients

Salt to rim glass (optional)
Ice
2 ounces reposado tequila of choice
1 ounce Cointreau
1 ounce fresh lime juice
1 ounce simple syrup
Lime garnish

1. Up: Shake ingredients with ice. Strain into a chilled cocktail glass.

2. Rocks: Shake ingredients with ice. Strain into a margarita glass filled with ice.

3. Frozen: Blend juice and syrup with a half cup of ice. Pour into a margarita glass. Top with the alcohol. Stir.

Top-shelf Margarita

Ingredients

Salt to rim glass (optional)
Ice
2 ounces reposado tequila of choice
½ ounce Cointreau
½ ounce Grand Marnier
1 ounce fresh lime Juice
1 ounce simple syrup
Lime garnish

1. Up: Shake ingredients with ice. Strain into a chilled cocktail glass.

2. Rocks: Shake ingredients with ice. Strain into a margarita glass filled with ice.

3. Frozen: Blend juice and syrup with a half cup of ice. Pour into a margarita glass. Top with the alcohol. Stir.

Basically, *gold tequila* is a marketing term that means a category of tequila called "joven." Jovens are just blanco tequilas that have had fake coloring added to make them look gold. Consumers then think that they are purchasing aged tequila because aging in barrels is what turns spirits amber gold. The most popular joven is Jose Cuervo.

Cointreau is the best orange liqueur. Grand Marnier is an orange liqueur as well but with a cognac base.

· · · · · · · · · GREEN ● LIGHT · · · · · · · · ·

If you love your margarita frozen/blended, then the best way to make it is to blend only the nonalcoholic portion, pour it into the glass, leaving room at the top, then pour the alcohol portion on top. Blending requires ice, which is just frozen water, so the flavor of the quality tequila gets watered down when you blend it.

Millionaire Margarita

Ingredients

Edible gold flake salt to rim glass
Ice
2 ounces Clase Azul Ultra Tequila
1 ounce Grand Marnier Cuvée Speciale Cent Cinquantenaire
1 ounce fresh organic lime juice
1 ounce simple syrup

1. Up: Shake ingredients with ice. Strain into a chilled cocktail glass.

2. Rocks: Shake ingredients with ice. Strain into a margarita glass filled with ice.

3. Frozen: Blend juice and syrup with a half cup of ice. Pour into a margarita glass. Top with the alcohol. Stir.

Royal Tequila

Grand Marnier Cuvée Speciale Cent Cinquantenaire is made with fifty-year-old cognac sealed by hand in a hand-painted bottle. It sells for about $225. Not in your budget? Then buy the Cuvée du Centenaire. It's made with twenty-five-year-old cognac and sells for about $175. The Clase Azul Ultra Tequila sells for about $1,200 a bottle.

FRUITY MARGARITAS
Incorporate flavored liqueur, puree, and more in a basic margarita for fruity versions

Adding an extra flavor to the simple and basic recipe of a margarita adds fun and flair. These fruity flavors are found in almost every bar across America. Injecting the extra fruity flavor can be done in many ways. The flavor can come from juices, fruits, purees, nectars, liqueurs, and even flavored tequilas. Flavors that work well in a margarita are strawberry,

raspberry, melon, peach, mango, coconut, orange, and pineapple.

If you are using a flavored liqueur as your flavoring agent, then simply replace the orange liqueur with the flavored liqueur. When using all other flavorings, you keep the orange liqueur in the recipe. If you use a flavored liqueur, flavored

Strawberry Mix

Strawberry liqueurs are rarely used in a strawberry margarita. Most bars don't stock them, and most liquor stores don't carry them. Learn to make homemade strawberry purée in Chapter 19. Homemade strawberry mix can be found on page 93. Or use lots of fresh, ripe strawberries and a little more simple syrup.

Strawberry Margarita

Ingredients

Ice
2 ounces 100 percent blanco tequila of choice
1 ounce triple sec
1 ounce fresh lime juice
1 ounce simple syrup
2 ounces strawberry mix or puree
Lime and strawberry garnish

1. Blend ingredients with a half cup of ice. Add additional ice if needed.
2. Pour into a margarita glass. Add garnish.
3. You can replace the triple sec with Cointreau.

tequila, or juice in a fruity margarita, then you have the option to make them up, on the rocks, or frozen. When using purée and nectar flavors, you could make them up or on the rocks, but they work best when made frozen because they are thicker.

Normally you don't salt the rim on a fruity margarita; however, some people like the salt on a sweeter margarita. Others will rim the glass in sugar, and still others will make a 1:1 mixture of salt and sugar to rim with. The bottom line is preference.

Melon Margarita

Ingredients

Ice
2 ounces 100 percent blanco tequila of choice
1 ounce melon liqueur
$1/10$ ounce fresh lime juice
1 ounce simple syrup
Lime garnish

1. Blend ingredients with a half cup of ice. Add additional ice if needed.
2. Pour into a margarita glass. Add garnish.
3. You can replace the blanco tequila with reposado tequila.

Peach Margarita

Ingredients

Ice
2 ounces 100 percent blanco tequila
1 ounce triple sec
$1/10$ ounce fresh lime juice
1 ounce simple syrup
2 ounces peach purée
$1/2$ ounce grenadine
Peach and lime garnish

1. Blend ingredients (except the grenadine) with a half cup of ice.
2. Pour grenadine into the bottom of the glass.
3. Pour the blended mixture into the glass. Add garnish.
4. You can replace the triple sec with Cointreau.

UNIQUE FRUITY MARGARITAS
Combine fruity flavors that complement each other for extra flavor and fun

Certain flavors simply blend together well. A great example is chocolate and peanut butter, but don't worry: You won't be making a chocolate-peanut butter margarita! Combining complementary flavors is the next progressive step to creating unique fruity margaritas. Don't limit yourself to the margaritas on this page because so many flavors mix well together in a margarita. Some examples are strawberry-kiwi, peach-papaya, blueberry-mint, mandarin-coconut, watermelon-pepper, and raspberry-lemon.

You can also find an assortment of infused and flavored tequilas with these flavors: coconut, pomegranate, citrus, coffee, chili, mango, almond, and berry. Of course, you can

Blue Coconut Margarita

Ingredients

Ice
2 ounces coconut Tequila
1 ounce blue Curacao
$1/10$ ounce fresh lime juice
1 ounce simple syrup
Shredded coconut rim for glass

1. Rim a margarita glass with shredded coconut.
2. Blend ingredients with a half cup of ice. Add additional ice if needed.
3. Pour into a margarita glass.

Pomegranate Mango Margarita

Ingredients

Ice
2 ounces reposado tequila
1 ounce triple sec
1 ounce fresh lime juice
1 ounce simple syrup
1 ounce mango puree
½ ounce pomegranate juice

1. Blend ingredients with a cup of ice. Add additional ice if needed.
2. Pour into a margarita glass.
3. You can replace the triple sec with Cointreau.

always infuse your own tequila by learning how in Chapter 19 (Techniques & Recipes).

As far as unique rims for margaritas, you can always make colored salt and flavored salt. To color the salt, simply put half a cup of coarse salt and one drop of food coloring into a plastic bag, then shake. Flavors can be added the same way by using extracts, syrups, juice, and citrus zest. You can also purchase colored salts. Other dry stocks can be mixed with the salt, too, such as chili powder, cinnamon, ground coffee, ground peppercorns, and edible gold and silver flake..

MAKE IT EASY

Rimming with coconut flakes requires a little more sticking power than does just rubbing a lemon or lime around the rim and then dipping. And even though simple syrup is very sticky, it's just not quite sticky enough. You'll have to use Karo light syrup. Pour an ounce of Karo syrup onto a saucer, squeeze one lime wedge, and mix together.

Sunrise Margarita

Ingredients

Ice
2 ounces reposado tequila
1 ounce triple sec
1 ounce fresh lime juice
1 ounce orange juice
1 ounce simple syrup
½ ounce grenadine

1. Fill a margarita glass with ice.
2. Shake ingredients (except the grenadine) with ice.
3. Strain into the glass. Add grenadine.
4. You can replace the triple sec with Cointreau.

Mexican Wedding

The Sunrise Margarita is a great marriage of two of the most popular tequila drinks in the world: tequila sunrise and a margarita. Both came out of Mexico, and each has a list of people claiming to be its inventor. They were also huge hits in the 1970s after the Eagles and Jimmy Buffett mentioned them in hit songs.

AROUND-THE-WORLD MARGARITAS

Sip your margarita with flavors and liqueurs that can be found around the globe

Global themed margaritas can be great to serve at theme parties or just to have fun creating new ones! Basically, you are just adding an ingredient that represents a country, city, state, province, region, town, county, village, district, borough, hamlet, kingdom . . . well, you get the point.

What makes a Hawaiian Margarita Hawaiian is the pine-

apple and papaya because both are grown in Hawaii. You can replace the papaya with other Hawaiian fruits such as banana, coconut, or mango. This margarita can be served at a tiki-, tropical-, or luau-themed party. Feel free to garnish the drink with plenty of edible flowers and paper parasols.

The Italian Margarita uses the very sweet and romantic Dis-

KNACK BARTENDING BASICS

Hawaiian Margarita

Ingredients

Ice
2 ounces 100 percent agave blanco tequila
1 ounce triple sec
1 ounce fresh lime juice
1 ounce pineapple juice
1 ounce papaya puree
½ ounce simple syrup
Pineapple garnish

1. Up: Shake ingredients with ice. Strain into a chilled cocktail glass.

2. Rocks: Shake ingredients with ice. Strain into a margarita glass filled with ice.

3. Frozen: Blend ingredients with a half cup of ice. Pour into a margarita glass.

Italian Margarita

Ingredients

Ice
2 ounces 100 percent agave tequila of choice
1 ounce DiSaronno Originale Amaretto
1 ounce fresh lime juice
½ simple syrup
Pineapple garnish

1. Up: Shake ingredients with ice. Strain into a chilled cocktail glass.

2. Rocks: Shake ingredients with ice. Strain into a margarita glass filled with ice.

3. Frozen: Blend all but Amaretto with a half cup of ice. Pour into a margarita glass. Top with Amaretto. Stir.

aronno Originale. What makes it so romantic? Well, in 1525 an artist who studied under Leonardo da Vinci was commissioned to paint a fresco in the Basilica of Santa Maria delle Grazie in Saronno, Italy. His name was Bernardino Luini, and the fresco is entitled Adoration of the Magi. Luini chose a beautiful Italian girl to model for the Madonna, which was the subject of the fresco. She fell in love with Luini and created a liqueur made with brandy, apricot kernels, and other secret spices as a gift. She created DiSaronno Originale.

Southern Margarita

Ingredients

Ice
2 ounces reposado tequila
1 ounce Southern Comfort (SoCo)
1 ounce fresh lime juice
1 ounce simple syrup
Lime garnish

1. Up: Shake ingredients with ice. Strain into a chilled cocktail glass.
2. Rocks: Shake ingredients with ice. Strain into a margarita glass filled with ice.
3. Frozen: Blend all but SoCo with a half cup of ice. Pour into a margarita glass. Top with the SoCo. Stir.

French Margarita

Ingredients

Ice
2 ounces reposado tequila
1 ounce Chambord
1 ounce fresh lime juice
1 ounce simple syrup
Lime garnish

1. Up: Shake ingredients with ice. Strain into a chilled cocktail glass.
2. Rocks: Shake ingredients with ice. Strain into a margarita glass filled with ice.
3. Frozen: Blend ingredients with a half cup of ice. Pour into a margarita glass. Add more Chambord if desired.

CREATIVE MARGARITAS

Get more creative to bump up the "wow" factor

After you've mastered the basic—but still yummy—margarita, you can add flair with fun fruit flavors. But don't stop there! You can bump it up a notch by making some creative margaritas. You know it's a creative margarita when you look at the name and do a double-take: "Huh? A Jalapeño Marmalade Margarita?" The double-take reaction is all the measurement you need when you tell a friend about your new creation.

Here are some creative margarita ideas to provide a spring-board: Make a Mango Key Lime Pie Margarita using key lime juice in place of the lime juice and mango tequila. Make a Beer Belly Margarita using beer. Make a Watermelon Mojito Margarita using mint and frozen watermelon pieces, an Apple Pie Margarita using Tuaca and apple juice, an Apricot Prickly Pear Margarita using prickly pear juice, a Blood Orange Cinnamon Margarita, a Bananas Foster Margarita using a banana or banana liqueur and then lighting the floating

Tequila Rose

Tequila Rose is a tequila-based strawberry cream liqueur. It tastes a little like melted strawberry ice cream, so this margarita will taste like a creamy strawberry margarita. The drink will turn out pink in color. The color of rose petals used as a fun garnish is up to you or what you have available. Make sure to wash them.

Bed of Roses Margarita

Ingredients

Ice
1 ounce reposado tequila
2 ounces Tequila Rose liqueur
1 ounce fresh lime juice
½ ounce simple syrup
Rose petals and lime garnish

1. Blend ingredients with a half cup of ice.
2. Pour into a margarita glass. Add garnish.
3. You can also rim the glass with shredded rose petals if desired.

Grand Marnier (drink only when the flame dies out), or a Piñata Margarita that's layered with three different-colored margaritas (try regular/lime, peach, and strawberry) and garnished with an assortment of fun fruits (maybe even candy!) to carry on the piñata theme. Try them at a fiesta or Cinco de Mayo party!

Guacamole Margarita

Ingredients

Salt to rim glass
Ice
2 ounces reposado tequila
1 ounce Cointreau
½ ounce fresh lime juice
½ ounce fresh lemon juice
1 ounce simple syrup
½ ripe avocado (plus ½ for garnish)

Avocado slice, and cilantro sprig garnish

1. Rim a margarita glass with salt.
2. Blend ingredients with a half cup of ice.
3. Pour into a margarita glass. Add garnish. Garnish can include a lime slice as well.

Jalapeño Marmalade Margarita

Ingredients

Ice
2 ounces reposado tequila
1 ounce Grand Marnier or Cointreau
1 ounce fresh lime juice
1 ounce orange marmalade
½ jalapeño or whole if you like the heat
Whole jalapeño garnish

1. Blend ingredients with a cup of ice. Add additional ice if needed.
2. Pour into a margarita glass. Add garnish.
3. You can add more fresh lime juice to taste.

DAIQUIRIS

Learn the foundation of a daiquiri, then build upon it to create your own

Like the margarita, the daiquiri has a simple foundation based on minimal ingredients: rum, fresh lime juice, and simple syrup. The daiquiri is of Cuban descent (there's a town named "Daiquiri"), and as you might have guessed, many people claim to have invented the drink. As far as we know the term was first seen in print in 1898.

Today most people think that the definition of daiquiri is "frozen drink." This is untrue. Yes, a daiquiri can be made frozen, but it must have all three of the base ingredients. So, for example, you can never define a piña colada as a daiquiri because it does not contain lime juice.

To make flavored mixes, all you need are five things: the fruit

Classic Daiquiri

Ingredients

Ice
1½ ounces light Cuban rum
1 ounce fresh squeezed lime juice
½ ounce simple syrup

1. Chill a 4–6-ounce cocktail glass with ice.
2. Shake ingredients with ice.
3. Strain into the chilled cocktail glass.

Frozen Daiquiri

Ingredients

Ice
2 ounces light Cuban rum
2 ounces fresh squeezed lime juice
2 ounces simple syrup
Lime garnish

1. Blend ingredients with a half cup of ice. Add additional ice if needed.
2. Pour into stemmed glass.
3. Add garnish.

(or fruits) of choice, water, sugar, lime juice, and a blender. It's easy! Let's say you want to make Strawberry Daiquiri mix. (1) Take 2 cups of sugar and 2 cups of lukewarm water and shake in a jar. Let the cloudiness go away, then shake again until all the sugar has dissolved in the water. Set aside. (2) Squeeze a cup of lime juice. Set aside. (3) Cut the tops off 4 cups of ripe strawberries, then wash well or you can also use frozen strawberries. (4) Everyone has a different-size blender (and strawberries are different sizes), so you may have to make the mix in batches. Fill your blender with half the strawberries, then pour in half of the lime juice and half of the sugar water and blend. Your goal is to keep adding and blending ingredients to make a pourable mix. Taste as you go. You may not need all the sugar water, depending on the ripeness of the strawberries. Yields a half gallon. Pour into a container and keep in the fridge.

Strawberry Daiquiri

Ingredients

Sugar to rim glass (optional)
Ice
2 ounces light rum
4 ounces strawberry daiquiri mix
Choice of lime, strawberry, or whipped cream garnish

1. Blend ingredients with a half cup of ice. Add additional ice if needed.
2. Pour into stemmed glass.
3. Add preferred garnish. If sugar rim is your choice, then make that step 1.

Flavored Daiquiris

Flavored daiquiris are very popular. The most popular is a Strawberry Daiquiri. The next-most popular are peach, raspberry, mango, and banana. Also there are a lot of flavored rums to incorporate into a Classic Daiquiri, such as coconut, orange, raspberry, lemon, spiced, cherry, pineapple, banana, and mango. This is the easiest way to incorporate extra flavor into a daiquiri.

93

PIÑA COLADAS
Make the creamy, dreamy drink that instantly conjures a tropical state of mind

Mexico has the margarita, Cuba has the daiquiri, and Puerto Rico has the Piña Colada. This frozen libation is sung about, seen in films, and dreamt about by nine-to-five cubicle rat race workers on a daily basis.

The term Piña Colada is Spanish for *"strained pineapple."* And, of course, as you suspected, there's a line of people claiming to have invented the drink. The term was first seen in print in 1920, but the creamy version we have today wasn't available until the early 1950s, when Coco López coconut cream was invented. Before that, bartenders used coconut milk and shook and *strained* it (most times into coconut cups for tourists). The invention of the coconut cream allowed the Piña

Piña Colada

Ingredients

Ice
2 ounces Puerto Rican rum
1 ounce coconut cream
3 ounces pineapple juice
Pineapple flag garnish

1. Blend ingredients with a half cup of ice. Add additional ice if needed.
2. Pour into a tropical glass.
3. Add garnish.

Miami Vice

Ingredients

Ice
2 ounces light rum
1 ounce coconut cream
3 ounces pineapple juice
4 ounces strawberry daiquiri mix
Pineapple and strawberry garnish

1. Blend the first three ingredients with a half cup of ice.
2. Pour into a tropical glass.
3. Blend the strawberry daiquiri mix with a half cup of ice.
4. Pour into the glass. Add garnish.

Colada to be blended. Tip: Shake the can before opening because the solids and liquids inside separate.

You can compare the Piña Colada with the margarita and daiquiri again because its simplicity allows an imagination of flavors to enhance it. For example, just using different rums introduces a depth of flavor. Dark rums that contain molasses make the Piña Colada taste like heaven. Many people like to float the dark rum on top or just add it to the blending process. There are many gold, aged, and flavored rums to substitute for the light rum.

MAKE IT EASY

If you plan on making a few Piña Coladas for friends and family, then make it easy by premixing a Piña Colada mix. All you need is a pitcher, pineapple juice, and Coco López coconut cream. Fill the pitcher three-quarters full with pineapple juice and then the rest of the way with coconut cream and stir.

Melon Colada

Ingredients

Ice
1 ounce light rum
1 ounce melon liqueur
1 ounce coconut cream
3 ounces pineapple juice
Pineapple and cherry garnish

1. Blend ingredients with a half cup of ice. Add additional ice if needed.
2. Pour into a tropical glass.
3. Add garnish.

Flavored PC

You can add fun flavor by adding a liqueur. Other liqueurs that taste great in a Piña Colada are coffee, raspberry, chocolate, banana, peach, and Amaretto. For a fun color, float blue Curaçao on top, and for a lava look, simply pour a colored mix like strawberry into the bottom of the glass before you pour in the Piña Colada.

POST-PROHIBITION TROPICAL DRINKS
Try making some world-renowned drinks that will live on forever

Prohibition in America ended on December 5, 1933, at 3:32 p.m. Wow, what a party that must've been! One New Orleans speakeasy owner, Pat O'Brien, closed down his speakeasy, moved ten blocks to the French Quarter, and opened his doors for business. A major issue at this time was that whiskey was in short supply. This was due to the whiskey distilleries having been closed for thirteen years; also, whiskey takes time to age. Rum was abundant, so if a bar owner wanted a

case of whiskey he had to buy up to fifty cases of rum. That's how the Hurricane was born; huge hurricane glasses were filled with lots of rum and juices for tourists and sailors.

Donn the Beachcomber, a bootlegger in New Orleans during Prohibition, decided to leave Cajun country to open the first tiki bar in Hollywood. He invented the first pu pu platter and many tiki drinks, with the Zombie being the most popular. The Zombie was served at the 1939 New York World's Fair.

Hurricane

Ingredients

Ice
2 ounces light rum
2 ounces dark rum
2 ounces red passion fruit syrup
1 ounce orange juice
1 ounce pineapple juice
1 ounce fresh lime juice

Pineapple or orange flag garnish

1. Fill a hurricane glass with ice.
2. Shake ingredients with ice.
3. Strain into the glass. Add garnish

Zombie

Ingredients

1 ounce gold rum
1 ounce 151 Demerara rum
1 ounce light rum
1 ounce lemon juice
1 ounce lime juice
1 ounce pineapple juice
1 ounce passion fruit syrup
1 teaspoon brown sugar
1 dash Angostura bitters

Ice
Mint sprig garnish

1. Pour everything into a shaker tin without ice and stir until the sugar dissolves. Add ice, then shake and strain into the glass—a tiki or tall glass.
2. Add garnish.

Trader Vic owned a small grocery in San Francisco and worked as a waiter. He opened a tiki bar across the street from his grocery store and invented the Mai Tai. He was the first to open a chain of tiki bars.

ZOOM

The term mai tai is Tahitian for "out of this world." The original recipe is slightly different from the recipe created for the Trader Vic's chain due to availability of products. When bartenders not working at Trader Vic's are asked to duplicate the recipe, they are limited to the standard products behind their bars, a limitation that begat the Copycat Mai Tai.

Trader Vic Mai Tai

Ingredients

Ice
1 ounce aged Jamaican rum (like Appleton's)
1 ounce amber Martinique rum (like St. James or Clément)
½ ounce orange Curaçao
½ ounce orgeat syrup (French almond syrup)
½ ounce fresh lime juice
1 ounce Trader Vic's rock candy syrup (or commercial simple syrup)
Mint sprig garnish

1. Fill a double old-fashioned glass with ice.
2. Shake ingredients with ice.
3. Strain into the glass. Add garnish.

Copycat Mai Tai

Ingredients

Ice
½ ounce triple sec
½ ounce Amaretto
2 ounces sweet-and-sour mix
2 ounces pineapple juice
1 ounce light rum
1 ounce dark rum
Pineapple and cherry garnish

1. Fill a tropical glass with ice.
2. Shake ingredients (except the dark rum) with ice.
3. Strain into the glass.
4. Float dark rum on top. Add garnish.

FROZEN & TROPICAL DRINKS

GLOBAL TROPICAL DRINKS
Make frozen and tropical drinks from popular tourist destinations

In the 1950s, Hawaii went through a phase of exotic paradise construction to attract tourists. Tropical getaways were being built on every island, and the largest of these was the Hawaiian Village on the island of Oahu. Harry Yee, a veteran bartender working at the Hawaiian Village, was asked by Bols to help promote its Blue Curaçao, and the Blue Hawaii was born. When asked about the orchid garnish, his answer was, "We used to use a sugarcane stick, and people would chew

on the stick, then put it in the ashtray. When the ashes and cane stuck together it made a real mess, so I put the orchids in the drink to make the ashtrays easier to clean."

Yee not only was the first to put an orchid into a drink but also was the first to put a paper parasol into a drink and even a Chinese back scratcher into a drink, which he called a "tropical itch." There are just too many of his drinks to mention, but just know that at the time there weren't any "Hawaiian drinks,"

Blue Hawaii

Ingredients

Ice
¾ ounce Puerto Rican rum
¾ ounce vodka
½ ounce Bols blue Curaçao
3 ounces pineapple juice
1 ounce sweet-and-sour mix
Orchid garnish

1. Fill a tropical glass with ice.
2. Shake ingredients with ice.
3. Strain into the glass.
4. Add garnish.

Blue Hawaiian

Ingredients

Ice
1 ounce light rum
½ ounce blue Curaçao
3 ounces pineapple juice
1 ounce sweet-and-sour mix
Pineapple flag garnish

1. Fill a tropical glass with ice.
2. Shake ingredients with ice.
3. Strain into the glass.
4. Add garnish.
5. Shake all the ingredients with ice, then strain into tropical glass with ice.

so he was the one responsible for lighting this fire. The Blue Hawaiian is a spinoff Harry's Blue Hawaii minus the orchid and vodka. If you ask for this drink in any bar today, this is the version you will receive.

The Singapore Sling was created at the Raffles Hotel in Singapore at the turn of the twentieth century by Chinese bartender Ngiam Tong Boon to attract women, so it was one hundred years ahead of the cosmopolitan in that respect.

No one knows who invented the Bahama Mama, but it came from the Bahamas in the 1980s. It can be made many ways with many ingredients as long as you keep the same flavor profile, which is a cross between a Piña Colada and a Rum Punch.

Singapore Sling

Ingredients

Ice
1½ ounces gin
½ ounce Peter Herring Cherry Heering
¼ ounce Cointreau
¼ ounce Benedictine
2 ounces pineapple juice
1 dash Angostura bitters
¼ ounce grenadine

½ ounce lime juice
2 ounces soda water
Pineapple or orange flag garnish

1. Fill a tropical glass with ice.
2. Shake ingredients (except soda water) with ice.
3. Strain into the glass. Add soda water.
4. Add garnish.

Bahama Mama

Ingredients

Ice
1 ounce coconut rum
1 ounce light rum
2 ounces orange juice
2 ounces pineapple juice
½ ounce grenadine
Pineapple or orange flag garnish

1. Rocks: Shake ingredients with ice. Strain into a tropical glass filled with ice. Add garnish.

2. Frozen: Blend ingredients with a half cup of ice. Pour into a tropical glass. Add garnish.

ANIMAL-INSPIRED TROPICAL DRINKS
These concoctions are guaranteed to be more fun than a barrel of monkeys

Animal names for drinks have always been very popular. With a little research one can find names such as Grasshopper, Moscow Mule, Horse's Neck, Monkey Gland, Greyhound, Salty Dog, and Scorpion.

It's safe to assume that any drink with the word monkey in the name will involve banana. The Chocolate Monkey is a base recipe for you to start with. Much can be substituted just as long as you keep the banana/chocolate balance. For example, in place of the vanilla vodka you could use chocolate vodka, banana vodka, or banana rum. Let your imagination go wild! For a garnish, you could use chocolate whipped cream, chocolate sprinkles, shredded chocolate, or banana-shaped candy.

Chocolate Monkey

Ingredients

Chocolate syrup
1 ounce vanilla vodka
1 ounce banana liqueur
1 ounce white crème de cacao
4 ounces half-and-half
Ice
Whipped cream garnish

1. Squirt some chocolate syrup into a tall glass.
2. Blend ingredients with a half cup of ice. Add additional ice if needed.
3. Pour into the glass. Add garnish.

Frog in a Blender

Ingredients

Chocolate syrup
½ ounce grenadine
1 ounce white crème de cacao
1 ounce green crème de menthe
4 ounces half-and-half
Ice
Whipped cream garnish

1. Squirt some chocolate syrup into a tall glass.
2. Pour grenadine into the glass.
3. Blend remaining ingredients with a half cup of ice.
4. Pour into the glass. Add garnish.

So far there's not any solid evidence for the origin of the Yellowbird. What we do know is that in 1957 Alan and Marilyn Bergman wrote the lyrics for song "The Yellow Bird" to an 1883 Haitian tune. Now let's fly to Hawaii, where Arthur Lyman—king of tiki lounge exotica music—recorded the song (which shot to number four on the Billboard charts in 1961). Well, it just so happens that Lyman played weekly in the Shell Bar at the Hawaiian Village (think bartender Harry Yee/Blue Hawaii). So it's possible that the drink was invented in Hawaii.

· · · · · · · · · GREEN ● LIGHT · · · · · · · · ·

The Frog in a Blender is a novelty frozen drink. It tastes like a fresh peppermint patty, but it can easily jump all the way to the other end of the spectrum if you insert a rubber frog halfway into the drink and then serve. It's perfect to serve at Halloween! To bump up the alcohol level, add vodka or chocolate vodka.

Yellowbird

Ingredients

Ice
1 ounce light rum
1 ounce Galliano
½ ounce banana liqueur
2 ounces pineapple juice
2 ounces orange juice

1. Fill a tall glass with ice.
2. Shake ingredients with ice.
3. Strain into the glass.

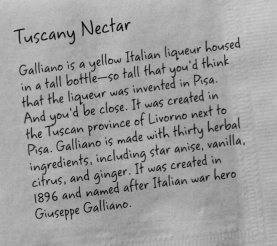

Tuscany Nectar

Galliano is a yellow Italian liqueur housed in a tall bottle—so tall that you'd think that the liqueur was invented in Pisa. And you'd be close. It was created in the Tuscan province of Livorno next to Pisa. Galliano is made with thirty herbal ingredients, including star anise, vanilla, citrus, and ginger. It was created in 1896 and named after Italian war hero Giuseppe Galliano.

FROZEN & TROPICAL DRINKS

FROZEN DESSERT DRINKS

Trade your spoon for a spoon straw and enjoy a favorite dessert in a glass

This is where you can really have some fun. The first question to ask is, "What are my favorite desserts?" because practically any dessert can be turned into a dessert drink. So what is it? Maybe the thought sent your brain on a sugar rush, and it's spinning a little right now, so take a breath and break it down. How about cakes? Do you like any of these: devil's

food, red velvet, carrot, black forest, pineapple upside-down, or wedding cake?

What about pie flavors such as lemon meringue, pecan, pumpkin, custard, coconut cream, key lime, or peach? Maybe you're a cookie person. How about chocolate chip, oatmeal, applecinnamon, macaroons, Oreos, gingersnaps, or thin mints?

Banana Cream Pie

Ingredients

Karo syrup to paint glass
Crushed graham cracker
1 ounce vanilla vodka
1 ounce banana liqueur
½ ounce butterscotch schnapps
Half a banana
4 ounces half-and-half
Ice

Whipped cream garnish

1. Paint half the inside of a tall glass with Karo syrup.
2. Sprinkle with graham cracker crumbs.
3. Blend ingredients with a half cup of ice.
4. Pour into the glass. Add whipped cream garnish.

Strawberry Shortcake

Ingredients

Whipped cream
1 ounce vodka
1 ounce Amaretto
2 ounces half-and-half
2 ounces strawberry mix
Ice
Strawberry garnish

1. Squirt whipped cream into the bottom of a tall glass.
2. Blend ingredients with a half cup of ice.
3. Pour into the glass. Add whipped cream garnish.

The whole point is to spark your imagination. With all the flavored spirits, liqueurs, and mixers available, the possibilities are endless. You simply break down the key elements of the recipe. For example, if you read a recipe for Banana Cream Pie, you'll see that the recipe calls for bananas, milk, sugar, butter, vanilla, and a whipped cream topping. So you can use vanilla vodka, banana liqueur, butterscotch schnapps, half-and-half, and some fresh banana to give it some body. Blend it up, then top it whipped cream. Voilá!

German Chocolate Cake

Ingredients

Shredded coconut and chocolate syrup
1 ounce coconut rum
1 ounce dark crème de cacao
½ ounce hazelnut liqueur
1 scoop chocolate ice cream
1 ounce half-and-half
Ice

Whipped cream, and chocolate shavings garnish

1. Rim a tall glass with chocolate syrup and shredded coconut.
2. Blend ingredients with a half cup of ice.
3. Pour into the glass. Add garnish.

Place Your Bet

If you bet that German Chocolate Cake originated in Germany and was created by a stout German woman in her kitchen, well, you'd lose. A Texas homemaker who sent the recipe to her local newspaper in 1957 created it. The recipe used Baker's German Sweet Chocolate, a brand created by an Englishman in 1852.

FROZEN & TROPICAL DRINKS

103

TEQUILA-BASED SHOTS
Here are the shots that will shoot you south of the border the fastest

Before cocktails, there were shots. It was simple, really: a shot of hard liquor alongside a brew. And even though things change through time it's funny how they stay the same. I bet those cowboys sitting at dusty tables in local saloons never knew how hip it was to order a bottle for the table. Today they call it "bottle service," and it can be found in trendy nightclubs the world over. And although spots have changed in flavor, color, and names, the purpose remains the same.

A plain ol' Shot of Tequila will probably never go out of style. There will just be new ways of shooting it. The most common way today is the lick it, slam it, suck it method. You lick some salt, then drink the tequila and suck on a lime. A lemon can be used, too, if that's your preference. Also using the salt and the lime to help you get the tequila down your throat is often referred to as using "training wheels."

In some countries, people substitute the salt for cinnamon

Shot of Tequila

Ingredients

Lime (or lemon) slice
salt to rim glass
1½ ounces tequila of choice

1. Wet part of a shot glass with a lime slice, then dip it in salt.
2. Pour tequila into the glass.
3. Lick the salt, drink the tequila, then bite into the meat of the lime.

Prairie Fire

Ingredients

1½ ounces tequila of choice
5 dashes Tabasco

1. Pour the tequila into a shot glass
2. Dash in five hard jerks of Tabasco.

and the lime for orange when shooting aged tequila. And around the millennium, the trendy way to shoot tequila is chilled, which is another way to avoid tasting the tequila.

A dash of Tabasco helps mask the taste of tequila.

Bull Fight

Ingredients

5 ounces coffee liqueur
½ ounce Sambuca
½ ounce gold tequila
2 dashes Tabasco

1. Slowly layer the first three ingredients in order into a shot glass.
2. Dash the Tabasco.

Flat Tire

Ingredients

¾ ounce black Sambuca
¾ ounce tequila of choice
Ice

1. Shake the black Sambuca and tequila with ice.
2. Strain into a shot glass.

SHOTS

105

VODKA-BASED SHOTS
Make some bursting-with-flavor citrus shots that satisfy all

Everyone seems to like citrus-based shots, so you can't go wrong here. All of these need to be super chilled by shaking with ice; however, if you'd rather experience a fuller flavor, then keep the citrus vodka in the freezer and then just pour when ready.

If you want to add a fun twist to this Lemon Drop Shot, then dip half of a lemon wheel in sugar and the other half in ground espresso. Here's a top-shelf Lemon Drop Shot spinoff

that you can serve to your special guests. For each, you'll need 1½ ounces of chilled citrus vodka, ½ ounce of Grand Marnier, lemon slice, a teaspoon of sugar, a match, a saucer, and a shot glass. To start, lay the lemon slice on the saucer and cover with the sugar. Pour some Grand Marnier on top of the sugar to make it flammable, then light. As the sugar is being crystallized into the lemon, chill a shot of citrus vodka and pour it into the shot glass. By the time you're done, the

Lemon Drop Shot

Ingredients

Sugar to rim glass
1½ ounces citrus vodka
Ice

1. Rim a shot glass with sugar.
2. Shake vodka with ice.
3. Strain into the glass.

Russian Roulette

Ingredients

1½ ounces vodka
Ice
Orange slice
Sugar
¼ ounce 151 rum or Grand Marnier

1. Shake the vodka with ice and strain into a shot glass.
2. Place an orange slice on top of the glass with sugar and rum on top of the orange.
3. Light the orange, then wait until the flame dies out.
4. Pick up the orange, drink, and then bite the sugary, warm orange.

flame will have died down. Now drink the chilled shot, then bite into the warm, sugary lemon. Pick up the saucer and pour the leftover Grand Marnier into the shot glass and drink it, too. It's very decadent tasting.

Chocolate Cake

Ingredients

Ice
1 ounce lemon vodka
½ ounces Frangelico hazelnut liqueur
Sugared lemon wedge garnish

1. Shake the ingredients with ice.
2. Strain into a shot glass.
3. Drink, then bite into a lemon dipped in sugar.

Weird Cake

There's not any chocolate in the Chocolate Cake shot, but it tastes like it. This shot showed up around the millennium. It's one of those weird "Twilight Zone" mouth sensations. It uses citrus vodka, and hazelnut liqueur and ends with a sugared lemon. The weird part is that when you bite into the lemon, it tastes like chocolate cake. Weird.

SHOTS

LIQUEUR-BASED SHOTS
Try some sweet and creamy shots that pack a punch

The B-52 shot was named after the U.S. B-52 Stratofortress bombers built for the Air Force in 1954. President George H. W. Bush took them off alert duty in 1991. Many people have claimed to have created the shot, but the only real fact agreed upon so far is that its birth was in the 1970s. Grand Marnier was born in 1880, Kahlúa was born in 1936, but Baileys Original Irish Cream was not born until 1974.

You should know that names of shots were always pretty tame up until the 1980s. You see, America had just come out of the wild and free rock/disco explosion due to the ending of the Vietnam War, but then in 1981 a disease that no one had ever heard of permeated the world. It was called AIDS and it was frightening because no one knew what was causing it. Finally it was found to be a sexually transmitted disease. For the bar scene, this was a huge concern. Ever since women had been allowed into bars in the 1920s, bars

B-52

Ingredients

½ ounce Kahlúa coffee liqueur
½ ounce Baileys Original Irish Cream
½ ounce Grand Marnier

1. Layer the liqueurs in the order given into a shot glass.

Whipped Cream Shot

Ingredients

¾ ounce coffee liqueur
¾ ounce Irish cream
Whipped cream garnish

1. Slowly layer the two ingredients in order into a shot glass.
2. Top with whipped cream.
3. Drink without using your hands.

had had sexual undertones. Public anxiety grew, and many people were frustrated by not knowing what to do because having sex—the way they were used to—could mean dying. It was the collective frustration of not being able to act out sexually that conceived these drinks with provocative names. Bartenders were providing only what the public desired at that time. If people couldn't have sex, then, by golly, they would enjoy playful substitutions.

You can adjust liqueur portions to the size of the shot glass you are using.

Buttery Irishman

Ingredients

¾ ounce butterscotch schnapps
¾ ounce Irish cream

1. Pour the butterscotch schnapps into a shot glass.
2. Slowly layer the Irish cream on top of the schnapps.

Irish Cream Shots

Irish cream shots first started in 1974 and there are many other liqueurs that mix well with it. In the same way you layer the Irish cream on top of butterscotch schnapps to make a Buttery Irishman, you can replace the schnapps with Sambuca, crème de banana, or cinnamon schnapps.

109

SHOTS

WHISKEY-BASED SHOTS

Try some whiskey shots made from the Earth's amber waves of grain

The Three Wise Men shot was more than likely created by men tired of the sweet, girly shots from the 1980s and 1990s. The novelty of the shot strictly plays off the name of the particular alcohol used. This foundation recipe is pretty solid because a tower of shots can be built on top. For example, if you add Wild Turkey Bourbon, then the shot is called "Three

Wise Men Go Hunting." Add Jose Cuervo into the mix, and it turns into *Three Wise Men Go to Mexico.* You begin to see the pattern pretty quickly.

Here are more to try. *Three Wise Men Go Bananas* = add banana liqueur; *Three Wise Men Go Sailing* = add Captain Morgan spiced rum; *Three Wise Men Love Chocolate* = add chocolate

Three Wise Men

Ingredients

½ ounce Jack Daniel's Tennessee whiskey
½ ounce Johnnie Walker Scotch whisky
½ ounce Jim Beam Bourbon
Ice

1. Shake the three whiskeys with ice.
2. Strain into a shot glass.
3. Can be served neat as well.

Monkey on Jack's Back

Ingredients

¾ ounce banana liqueur
¾ ounce Jack Daniel's Tennessee whiskey

1. Pour the banana liqueur into a shot glass.
2. Slowly layer the Jack Daniel's on top of the liqueur.
3. Can be served chilled and up as well.

liqueur; *Three Wise Men Go Nutty* = add Amaretto; *Three Wise Men Go Goose Hunting with a Friend* = add Greygoose vodka and George Dickel Bourbon; *Three Wise Men Triple Date* = add brandy, ginger liqueur, and Tia Maria; and *Three Wise Men Strike Gold in Germany* = add Goldschlager and Jägermeister.

You can always insert an adjective as well, such as *Three Bitter Wise Men* = add a dash of bitters. Other words to try are buttery, blue, fuzzy, and hot.

Snowshoe

Ingredients

Ice
¾ ounce Wild Turkey Bourbon
¾ ounce peppermint schnapps

1. Shake the ingredients with ice.
2. Strain into a shot glass.

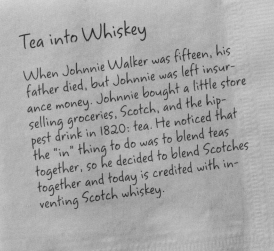

Tea into Whiskey

When Johnnie Walker was fifteen, his father died, but Johnnie was left insurance money. Johnnie bought a little store selling groceries, Scotch, and the hippest drink in 1820: tea. He noticed that the "in" thing to do was to blend teas together, so he decided to blend Scotches together and today is credited with inventing Scotch whiskey.

SHOTS

111

WORLD FLAG SHOTS
Try layering shots while traveling around the world

Some people may think it's disrespectful to marry flags and alcohol together, but it's not like we're burning any of these flags. Besides, every country has an official alcohol that represents that country. Mexico has tequila, the U.S. has bourbon, Ireland has Irish whiskey, England has gin, Portugal has port, Russia has vodka, Greece has ouzo, France has cognac, Norway has akvavit, and many Caribbean islands have rum. So, salud, cheers, a sua saude, a votre sante, and skaal!

The American Flag shot can also be called by its two nicknames, "Old Glory" and "Star-Spangled Banner." If you like the latter, then cut a star fruit and set it on the rim just for fun. This shot—when drunk in one gulp—tastes exactly like a chocolate-covered cherry. It's great for patriotic parties. If you stir it with a cocktail straw, then it turns purple, and you can say that you can see the purple mountain majesties.

The Mexican Flag shot is perfect for a fiesta or a Cinco de

American Flag

Ingredients

1¼ ounce white crème de cacao
Few drops of grenadine
¼ ounce blue Curacao

1. Pour the white crème de cacao into a shot glass.
2. Pour the grenadine in, and it will sink to the bottom.
3. Slowly layer the blue Curacao on top.

Mexican Flag

Ingredients

½ ounce grenadine
½ ounce green crème de menthe
½ ounce half-and-half

1. Pour the grenadine into a shot glass.
2. Slowly layer the green crème de menthe on top of the grenadine.
3. Slowly layer the half-and-half on top of the crème de menthe.

Mayo party. The colors of the Mexican flag (red, green, and white) have changed through the years, but today they mean hope, unity, and the blood of the national heroes.

Irish Flag

Ingredients

½ ounce green crème de menthe
½ ounce Irish cream
½ ounce Irish whiskey

1. Pour the green crème de menthe into a shot glass.
2. Slowly layer the Irish cream on top.
3. Slowly layer the Irish whiskey on top of the Irish cream.

Alaskan Flag

Ingredients

¾ ounce chilled Goldschlager cinnamon schnapps
¾ ounce blue Curacao

1. Pour the Goldschlager into a shot glass.
2. Slowly layer the blue Curacao on top.

SHOTS

NOVELTY SHOTS
Create some out-of-the-box shots to impress your friends

You can purchase pricey chocolate shot glasses, but why do that when you can make your own? You will need 3-ounce paper Dixie cups, 1-ounce plastic portion cups, a double boiler (or microwave), a cookie sheet, unflavored cooking spray, baking chocolate, and baker's wax. Amounts will vary, depending on how many you want to make, so just start with small batches at first to get the hang of it.

(1) Melt the chocolate and baker's wax in a double boiler or microwave. (2) Spray the insides of the 3-ounce cups and the outsides of the 1-ounce cups with the cooking spray to prevent sticking. (3) Pour the melted chocolate ¾ of the way up the 3-ounce cup, then push the 1-ounce cup into the chocolate until the chocolate oozes to the top. This molds the inside of the shot glass. (4) Place onto the cookie sheet, then place into the freezer to set up. (5) When ready, remove from the freezer and pop off the portion cups.

Pirate Treasure

Ingredients

¾ ounce chilled Goldschläger
¾ ounce chilled Captain Morgan spiced rum

1. Pour the Goldschläger into a shot glass.
2. Slowly layer the Captain Morgan spiced rum on top.

S'mores

Ingredients

½ ounce vanilla vodka or rum
¼ ounce butterscotch schnapps
¼ ounce Irish cream
1 Teddy Grahams bear for garnish
Splash 151 rum
2 minimarshmallows on a toothpick

Chocolate shot glass

1. Pour the first three ingredients into a chocolate shot glass.
2. Set the Teddy Grahams bear on top, then top with 151 rum. Light.
3. Roast marshmallows, blow out the flame.
4. Drink, bite chocolate glass, then eat the marshmallows.

114

The 1-ounce portion cups can be found at candy, wedding, and restaurant supply stores. Don't stop with chocolate! Try juices and other liquids. Just tape across the top of the cups to keep in place.

Twist it up by using colored mashmellows and while chocalate glasses.

Flu Shot

Ingredients

¾ ounce melon liqueur
¾ ounce Jägermeister
Ice

1. Shake the ingredients with ice.
2. Pour into a shot glass.

Give Your Best Shot

Be the life of the party or impress your friends by investing in some reusable plastic shooter syringes. Of course, you can fill a syringe with your choice of shots, but the flu shot fits the bill perfectly. Make a batch by multiplying the recipe. Place them in a bowl or bucket of ice so they stay chilled.

SHOTS

CLASSIC SHOOTERS
Add a little mixer to your shots and feel your taste buds jump for joy

Shots and shooters have two things in common: Both are drunk in one gulp, and both have the same alcohol content. The difference is that shots are 100 percent alcohol, and shooters have a mixer added to them. And shooters require a slightly larger glass because of the mixer and the water, which melts during shaking. Shooters fit best in 3–5-ounce glasses.

Tip: At a nightclub, it's best to order shots, not shooters (un-less money is no object). For some reason, around the millennium nightclub bartenders began shaking up shooters and pouring them into shot-sized glasses. The alcohol portion for a shot or shooter should be 1–1½ ounces. These bartenders are pouring 1–1½ ounces of alcohol into the shaker tin, adding a bunch of mixer, shaking, then straining out five to eight shots from that one portion. And they charge $5–$9 for each! It was never this way in the 1960s–1990s.

Lemon Drop Shooter

Melon Ball

Ingredients

Ice
Sugar to rim glass
1 ounce citrus vodka
½ ounce triple sec
½ ounce lemon juice
½ ounce simple syrup
Sugared lemon (optional)

1. Shake the ingredients with ice and strain into a 3–5-ounce sugar-rimmed shooter glass.

Ingredients

Ice
1 ounce vodka
½ ounce melon liqueur
1 ounce orange juice

1. Shake ingredients with ice.
2. Strain into a 3–5-ounce shooter glass.

116

Some people like to replace the orange juice with pineapple juice.

It's rumored that this way of serving shooters evolved after the "martini craze" of the late 1990s. Before that, bartenders would sometimes serve rounds of shooters in cocktail/martini glasses (mostly to women). So, really, the flavored sipping martinis of today are just the gulping shooters of yesterday.

SoCo Lime

Ingredients

Ice
1½ ounces Southern Comfort
½ ounce Rose's lime cordial

1. Shake ingredients with ice.
2. Strain into a 3–5-ounce shooter glass.

Old Is New

Members of the millennium J-Lo generation may think they were hip and trendy by combining Southern Comfort and lime juice and naming the result "SoCo and Lime," but if Janis Joplin were alive today she'd have a few things to say about that. She was drinking Southern Comfort and Lime in the 1960s and made it well known that it was her drink of choice.

KAMIKAZES

Learn to make this Japanese-inspired shooter, then add your own twist

Kamikaze is a Japanese word. Kami means "God/divine," and kaze means "wind." In the late 1200s, Mongolia tried to invade Japan, but a typhoon killed the Mongolian invaders. The Japanese interpreted the typhoon as a gift from God. The Kamikaze shooter, however, did not get its name from the typhoon.

In 1944, almost seven hundred years later, America and Ja-

pan were at war (World War II). Japan's main defense strategy was using kamikaze pilots, in other words, pilots on a divine suicide mission. Young kamikaze pilots would steer their explosives-filled planes straight down into American ships. In the end, Japan lost around 2,800 pilots who sank 34 ships and damaged 368. Almost five thousand American sailors

Kamikaze

Ingredients

Ice
1 ounce vodka
½ ounce triple sec
½ ounce Rose's lime cordial

1. Shake ingredients with ice.
2. Strain into a 3–5-ounce shooter glass.

Blue Kamikaze

Ingredients

Ice
1 ounce vodka
½ ounce blue Curacao
½ ounce Rose's lime cordial

1. Shake ingredients with ice.
2. Strain into a 3–5-ounce shooter glass.

were killed. The same number were wounded.

Today many things are named "kamikaze." There are video games, flying carnival rides, record labels, underground bands, Japanese comic books, and, of course, the shooter. The Kamikaze shooter is believed to have been named after the kamikaze pilots, not after the typhoon from the 1200s. No one knows who invented it when or where. Basically it's just a vodka gimlet with triple sec. And if you add cranberry juice, then you can call it a "cosmopolitan." These modern Kamikaze versions bump up the flavor value in a big way.

MAKE IT EASY

These flavored Kamikazes can jumpstart a world of possibilities because so many flavors go well with lime. Secondly, there are many flavored vodkas to choose from. You can also make *Rainbow Kamikazes* by secretly dropping one drop of food coloring into glasses. As you strain the Kamikazes into the glasses, your friends will be amazed how each drink comes out a different color.

Raspberry Kamikaze

Ingredients

Ice
1 ounce raspberry vodka
½ ounce Chambord
½ ounce Rose's lime cordial

1. Shake ingredients with ice.
2. Strain into a 3–5-ounce shooter glass.

Cherry Kamikaze

Ingredients

Ice
1 ounce cherry vodka
½ ounce triple sec
½ ounce Rose's lime cordial
Cherry garnish

1. Shake ingredients with ice.
2. Strain into a 3–5-ounce shooter glass. Add garnish.

RASPBERRY-BASED SHOOTERS
Go razzle-dazzle and shake up some delectable raspberry goodness

Raspberries have a decadent taste. You've probably seen the clamshells of them in the produce section with a sticker price to shock. The price throws them into the delicacy category. Simply put, raspberries don't taste sweet unless they are fully ripe. But soft and ripe don't travel well. The very best raspberries are the ones you find on a bush while strolling through the countryside. But even then a variety of birds has picked through the best ones.

There are a lot of raspberry liqueurs on the market, but Chambord Liqueur Royale de France is the ultimate raspberry liqueur. No other raspberry liqueur can compare with its taste. It has been made in the Loire River valley of France since the late 1600s with black raspberries, Madagascar vanilla, Moroccan citrus peel, honey, cognac, and, of course, some secret ingredients. It was a favorite drink for royal gatherings. The bottle is not like any other liqueur bottle in the world, with its

Add More Flavor

All three of these shooters came out of the 1980s before the flavored vodka craze, so feel free to experiment. For the *Purple Hooter* you could use half citrus vodka and half raspberry vodka. For the *Hollywood,* try pineapple and raspberry vodka. For the *Nuts and Berries,* know that you can substitute whole, 2 percent, 1 percent, skim, or soy milk.

Purple Hooter

Ingredients

Ice
1 ounce vodka
½ ounce raspberry liqueur
½ ounce lemon juice
½ ounce simple syrup

1. Shake ingredients with ice.
2. Strain into a 3–5-ounce shooter glass.

round shape adorned with a gold band, then topped with a gold crown cap. At the company Web site, chambordonline.com, you can find several wonderful drink recipes. The site also has Chambord cuisine recipes for hors d'oeuvres, salads, appetizers, entrees, and desserts.

MAKE IT EASY

If these shooters sound like they'd make a nice, tall, cool cocktail, you're right! All you have to do is fill a tall glass with ice, add the alcohol, fill with the mixer, and stir. It works the other way, too. Have a favorite cocktail? Well, make a shooter out of it by reducing the mixer amount.

Hollywood

Ingredients

Ice
1 ounce vodka
½ ounce raspberry liqueur
1 ounce pineapple juice

1. Shake ingredients with ice.
2. Strain into a 3–5-ounce shooter glass.

Nuts and Berries

Ingredients

Ice
1 ounce raspberry liqueur
1 ounce Frangelico
1 ounce half-and-half

1. Shake ingredients with ice.
2. Strain into a 3–5-ounce shooter glass.

CRANBERRY-BASED SHOOTERS
Whip up some sweet and tart shooters using a mixer born in the U.S.A.

Cranberries are indigenous to North America. Native Americans made a sweet sauce using cranberries and maple syrup. Although Cape Cod is known for cranberries, it's Wisconsin that produces half of the annual crop. Other states that grow cranberries include New Jersey, Oregon, and Washington.

Cranberries have been around a long time, but it wasn't until 1930 that the first cranberry juice was marketed. However, the juicer wasn't invented until the 1920s, so that invention may have played a part. In 1930, Ocean Spray introduced the commercial cranberry juice cocktail. Today you can find cranberry blends at your local grocery store in the following flavors: apple, cherry, grape, mango, raspberry, strawberry,

White Cranberry

White cranberries are harvested about three weeks before they turn red. White cranberry juice hit the market after the white grape industry came out with white grape juice. You can easily make a white Woo Woo by substituting regular cranberry juice for white cranberry juice. You can also find flavored white cranberry juice in peach and strawberry flavors.

Woo Woo

Ingredients

Ice
1 ounce vodka
1 ounce peach schnapps
1 ounce cranberry juice

1. Shake ingredients with ice.
2. Strain into a 3–5-ounce shooter glass.
3. You're supposed to drink this shooter, then yell, "Woo woo!"

and tangerine, which, by the way, opens a whole world of possibilities in substituting regular cranberry juice for any of the shooter recipes on this page.

The Scarlett O'Hara (Southern Comfort and cranberry juice with a lime) was the first popular cranberry cocktail. It was created for the 1939 film *Gone with the Wind*. The next popular cranberry cocktails didn't gain recognition until the 1970s: Cape Codder, Sea Breeze, and Bay Breeze. The reason for this delay was that the cranberry industry collapsed because the U.S. Department of Health announced that cranberry crops were tainted with toxic herbicides in 1959. By the 1980s, cranberry juice breathed new life into the cocktail world and spawned the Sex on the Beach and the Woo Woo. In the 1990s, cranberry juice hit a ball out of the park with the Cosmopolitan, and the new millennium brought us the Red Snapper and Red Headed German.

Red Snapper

Ingredients

Ice
1 ounce Crown Royal
1 ounce Amaretto
1 ounce cranberry juice

1. Shake ingredients with ice.
2. Strain into a 3–5-ounce shooter glass.

Red Headed German

Ingredients

Ice
1 ounce Jägermeister
1 ounce peach schnapps
1 ounce cranberry juice

1. Shake ingredients with ice.
2. Strain into a 3–5-ounce shooter glass.

LIQUEUR-BASED SHOOTERS
Surf your way to lunch with a monkey, and it will erase your mind

If not for Sidney E. Frank, the word Jägermeister would probably not be part of your vocabulary. He was the genius who imported and marketed this German herbal liqueur in the 1970s. And what better way to sell lots of product than to create a novelty machine to go with it! That's when the Jägermeister tap machine was born. This machine chills the Jäger to 28°F. It has been a huge success and is still going strong.

Oh, Sidney didn't stop there. Even though he was in his six-

ties during the 1980s, he knew that the key to marketing is to target pop culture. So he promoted Jäger by becoming the tour sponsor for Mötley Crüe, Metallica, and a list of underground bands. He then started the annual Jägermeister Music Tour.

In the 1990s, Sidney promoted Jäger by hiring models to become his Jägerdudes and Jägerettes. They rode around America on the fleet of Jäger Buses. He even created Jäger-

Surfer on Acid

Ingredients

Ice
1 ounce Jägermeister
½ ounce coconut rum
1 ounce pineapple juice

1. Shake ingredients with ice.
2. Strain into a 3–5-ounce shooter glass.

Monkey's Lunch

Ingredients

Ice
1 ounce banana liqueur
1 ounce coffee liqueur
1 ounce half-and-half

1. Shake ingredients with ice.
2. Strain into a 3–5-ounce shooter glass.

meister Trikes (Jäger Harley-Davidsons) to tour with the Jägermeister Music Tour and Band Program.

In 2000, Sidney was eighty-one years old, but that still didn't stop him. He lived long enough to promote the most explosive shooter of the millennium, the Jäger Bomb. He died in 2006.

ZOOM

Jägermeister was created in 1934 to serve medicinal purposes and to honor the forestry administration. This is why there is the head of a deer and a poem in German on the label. The word *Jägermeister* means "hunter-master" (Jäger = hunter, and meister = master). Jägermeister is made with fifty-six herbs, and most people think it tastes like cough medicine.

Mind Eraser

Ingredients

Ice
1 ounce coffee liqueur
½ ounce vodka
4 ounces soda water

1. Fill a highball glass with ice.
2. Pour the ingredients in order into the glass.
3. Drink fast with a straw.

Clean Slate

The Mind Eraser has been around since the 1980s. Its novelty lies in the fact that you drink it really fast through a straw. Some people put two straws together. You can give it a modern update by using flavored vodkas such as vanilla, chocolate, orange, or raspberry. You could also substitute the coffee liqueur for espresso liqueur to give it an extra kick.

BOILERMAKERS

Pour, drop, splash, and drink your way with the most popular Boilermakers

The Boilermaker started with two simple parts: a shot of whiskey followed by a chaser of beer. Then one day some man somewhere—probably after a hard day's work as a boilermaker—sat in the local bar and thought to himself, "I'm so tired that it would be much more efficient to just drop the shot in the beer, then drink it." And the Boilermaker was born.

Travelers now had a neat little bar room trick to show while they made their way by train and stagecoach from coast to coast. Of course, this is all speculation because no one knows the origin of the Boilermaker.

Today a Boilermaker has turned into a type of drink, the type in which you drop one liquid into another liquid, then

Irish Car Bomb

Ingredients

¾ ounce Irish whiskey
¾ ounce Baileys Original Irish Cream
6 ounces Guinness Stout

1. Pour the first two ingredients into a shot glass.
2. Pour the stout into a pint glass.
3. Drop the shot into the pint glass.

Lunch Box

Ingredients

¾ ounce Southern Comfort
¾ ounce Amaretto
3 ounces lager beer
3 ounces orange juice

1. Pour the first two ingredients into a shot glass.
2. Pour the beer and juice into a pint glass.
3. Drop the shot into the pint glass.

drink them both together. The most popular of these types are represented on this page.

The Irish Car Bomb is a yummy Boilermaker, but you should know that the Northern Irish take offense at the name of this American-made shooter because the Irish Republican Army killed nine innocent people and injured 130 civilians with car bombs in the summer of 1972. This event is known as "Bloody Friday." Likewise, Americans might be offended if people in other countries created a shooter called a "Twin Towers bomb" and then clinked their glasses and toasted.

Other Boilermakers you can try are a Sake Bomb (sake dropped into Japanese beer), Jackknife (Jack Daniel's dropped into beer), Canadian Car Bomb (Canadian whisky and maple syrup dropped into Canadian beer), and a Russian Ruffe (vodka dropped into beer).

Also, Tulane University students have been known to drop a shot of half citrus vodka and half blue Curaçao into a pilsner beer. The beer turns green, which matches their mascot, the Green Wave.

Flaming Dr Pepper

Ingredients

6 ounces lager beer
1 ounce amaretto
½ ounce 151 rum

1. Pour the beer into a pint glass.
2. Pour the other ingredients in order into a shot glass. Light.
3. Drop the flaming shot into the pint glass.

Jäger Bomb

Ingredients

1½ ounces Jägermeister
4 ounces Red Bull energy drink

1. Pour the Red Bull into a highball glass.
2. Pour the Jägermeister into a shot glass.
3. Drop the shot into the pint glass.

CLASSIC CHAMPAGNE COCKTAILS

Pop your way back in time by trying some historic champagne cocktails

The Champagne cocktail appeared in the very first cocktail recipe book, *How to Mix Drinks*, by Jerry Thomas in 1862. The cocktail has been seen in many films of the 1900s. Three are *Casablanca* in 1942, *An Affair to Remember* in 1957, and *Blast from the Past* in 1999.

Kir (rhymes with "ear") is made with crème de cassis (black-

currant liqueur) and white wine with a lemon twist. If you replace the white wine with Champagne, it's called a "kir Royale." It was named after French Mayor Canon Kir (of Dijon in Burgundy), who popularized the drink by promoting local products to help build the economy after World War II. He served it at every official event, especially when he had

Champagne Cocktail

Ingredients

1 sugar cube
5 dashes Angostura bitters
6 ounces brut Champagne
Lemon twist garnish

1. Soak a sugar cube with the bitters.
2. Drop the cube into a Champagne glass.
3. Pour in the Champagne. Add garnish.

Kir Royale

Ingredients

½ ounce crème de cassis
6 ounces brut Champagne
Lemon twist garnish

1. Pour the crème de cassis into a Champagne glass.
2. Pour in the Champagne. Add garnish.

international guests. Even though crème de cassis had been around since 1841, it was simply ordered as crème de cassis and white or crème de cassis and Champagne. It took one hundred years for it to have a name.

The French 75 first appeared in *The Savoy Cocktail Book* by Harry Craddock in 1930. It was named after a French 75-millimeter gun used in World War I.

MAKE IT EASY

When making cocktails with Champagne, it's important to chill as many ingredients as possible before they go into the glass—especially the Champagne! You can even chill the glasses ahead of time if you want. Also, because you are adding sweetness to the drinks with juices, liqueurs, and purees, it's best to use a dry/brut Champagne to balance.

French 75

Ingredients

Ice
1½ ounces gin
½ ounce lemon juice
½ ounce simple syrup
3 ounces brut Champagne
Lemon twist garnish

1. Shake the first three ingredients with ice.
2. Strain into a Champagne glass.
3. Pour in the champagne. Add garnish.

Spinoff Kirs

- Kir Imperial = Chambord + Champagne

- Cardinal = crème de cassis + red wine

- Kir Grand = Grand Marnier + Champagne

- Hibiscus Royale = Cranberry juice + peach liqueur + Champagne

- Elderflower Royale = Elderflower liqueur + Champagne

FRUIT CHAMPAGNE COCKTAILS

Adding fresh fruit juice, liqueur, and puree to champagne is always a hit

Two drinks are the most popular brunch cocktail: the Bloody Mary and the Mimosa. The Mimosa is believed to have been invented at the Hôtel Ritz in Paris in the 1920s. The Paris Ritz has been in many films, has been visited by royalty and celebrities (Hemingway was there so much that the hotel named one of the bars after him), was home to Coco Chanel

for thirty years, and was the last building that Diana, princess of Wales, ever set foot in minutes before her death.

Owner and bartender Arrigo Cipriani invented the Bellini in Venice at Harry's Bar in the 1930s. He named it after Italian artist Giovanni Bellini. Harry's is another bar frequented by celebrities, again including Hemingway! The drink was

Mimosa

Ingredients

2 ounces fresh squeezed orange juice
4 ounces Champagne
Strawberry garnish

1. Pour the juice into a Champagne glass.
2. Pour in the Champagne. Add garnish.

Hibiscus

Ingredients

2 ounces cranberry juice
4 ounces Champagne

1. Pour the juice into a Champagne glass.
2. Pour in the Champagne.

just for special occasions, but when it became a big hit Cipriani had the white peaches shipped in special. Of course, in a pinch you can make some yellow peach puree, but don't ever substitute the peach with peach liqueur. And don't substitute the prosecco with Champagne. Prosecco is an Italian sparkling wine with its own flavor. French Champagne does not pair well with the light, fruity flavor of the Bellini.

ZOOM

The Flirtini is from the TV show *Sex and the City*. It is mentioned at a New York City rooftop party when Samantha asks Carrie what she's drinking. Today you can twist it up by using pineapple vodka. One thing you don't want to do is shake and strain the vodka and pineapple juice first because the pineapple juice is too frothy.

Bellini

Ingredients

2 ounces white peach puree
4 ounces prosecco

1. Pour the puree into a Champagne glass.
2. Pour in the prosecco.

Flirtini

Ingredients

½ ounce vodka
1 ounce pineapple juice
4 ounces Champagne

1. Pour the vodka and juice into a Champagne glass.
2. Pour in the Champagne.

CELEBRITY CHAMPAGNE COCKTAILS
These famously fun libations will tickle your taste buds

American novelist Ernest Hemingway accomplished a lot in his lifetime. He won a Pulitzer Prize and a Nobel Prize. He also married four times and had three sons as well as traveled extensively. And while traveling he visited every famous bar along the way. And if the bar wasn't famous when he was there, it was when he left. While living in Key West he had the chance to visit Cuba (many times) and created his own twisted daiquiri appropriately named the "Hemingway Dai-

quiri" (grapefruit juice and Maraschino liqueur was added). He drank this drink at the historic bar Sloppy Joe's. While in England he created a Champagne cocktail called the "Hemingway Champagne," but it had another name as well: "Death in the Afternoon." He wrote a book by that title, and that was the time of day when he died in 1961.

Admiral Lord Nelson made such a name for himself that every October 21 in England he's remembered on Trafalgar Day.

Hemingway Champagne

Ingredients

2 ounces absinthe
4 ounces Champagne

1. Pour the absinthe into a Champagne glass.
2. Pour in the Champagne.

Admiral Nelson's Blood

Ingredients

1 ounce port (ruby)
4 ounces Champagne

1. Pour the port into a Champagne glass.
2. Pour in the Champagne.

At age twelve, he joined the navy. The year was 1771. By the time he was twenty years old, he had worked his way up to captain and soon bore the title of British admiral naval commander. The Battle of Trafalgar was his last victory. He was shot by sniper fire. The crew preserved his body in a barrel of rum so it would survive the voyage back to England. It's been said that by the time the ship made it back, the barrel was half empty because the crew kept taking sips of the rum. The rum in that barrel was dubbed Nelson's blood, a term that later lent itself to a Champagne cocktail.

If certain berries aren't in season yet, then use some frozen berries.

Marilyn Merlot

Ingredients

Ice
1 ounce Maraschino liqueur
3 ounces Marilyn Merlot red wine
3 ounces Champagne
Maraschino cherry garnish

1. Fill a wine glass half with ice.
2. Pour in the ingredients. Add garnish.

Halle Berry Bubbles

Ingredients

Ice
½ ounce blueberry vodka
½ ounce Chambord
5 ounces Champagne
Berries garnish

1. Fill a wine glass half with ice.
2. Pour in the ingredients. Add garnish.

UNIQUE CHAMPAGNE COCKTAILS

Combine yummy ingredients to add some uniqueness to your glass of bubbles

One of the unique things that everyone should know about Champagne is that you can't call it or label it "Champagne" unless it's made from the grapes grown in the Champagne region of France. All others must be called and labeled "sparkling wine." This is because of the nineteen years of Champagne Riots between 1908 and 1927. Basically, the issue was

about cheaper grapes being imported and then mixed with expensive grapes so the wine industry could sell more and therefore make more money. Rioters (five thousand of them at times) rampaged and destroyed the imported grapes and everything else in their path. Finally, in the summer of 1927, a French law was passed decreeing that all Champagne must

Unique Flavors

Unique flavors to try in your Champagne are melon liqueur and kiwi puree, tangerine and mandarin vodka, lychee liqueur and mango puree, peach bitters and passion fruit nectar, lavender syrup and lemon juice, pomegranate and watermelon juice, citrus vodka and strawberry puree, lemon juice and balls of orange sherbet, grape vodka and pineapple juice, and blue Curacao for blue Champagne.

Cherry Vanilla Fizz

Ingredients

Sugar to rim glass
Ice
½ ounce vanilla vodka
½ ounce grenadine
½ ounce lemon juice
5 ounces brut Champagne
Cherry garnish

1. Rim a Champagne glass with sugar.
2. Shake the first three ingredients with ice.
3. Strain into a Champagne glass.
4. Pour in the Champagne. Add garnish.

be made in the Champagne region of France.

Now you may be strolling through your local supermarket and notice that some California wines use the word Champagne on their label. How can this be? This can be because the winemakers were making the wine before the law was passed in 1927. Lots of American companies respected the French law and the hard work the growers did to get the law passed in France and changed their labels to read "sparkling wine" even though they didn't have to. But some obviously didn't care and decided to take full advantage of the loophole.

MAKE IT EASY

You can easily make your own candied ginger garnishes. All you need is 1 cup water, 1 cup sugar, and 1 cup peeled and chopped ginger pieces. Throw all of this onto the stove and simmer for 30 minutes. Strain, then lay out the pieces to dry (30 minutes), then sprinkle a little more sugar on them.

Violet Pear Sparkle

Ingredients

1 ounce Parfait Amour
1 ounce lemon pear puree
4 ounces brut Champagne
Edible flower garnish

1. Pour the first two ingredients into a coupe Champagne glass.
2. Pour in the Champagne. Add garnish.

Blood Orange Ginger Champagne

Ingredients

Ice
1 ounce Domaine de Canton French Ginger Liqueur
1 ounce blood orange juice
6 ounces brut Champagne
Candied ginger skewer garnish

1. Fill a wine glass half with ice.
2. Pour in the ingredients. Add garnish.

PINK CHAMPAGNE COCKTAILS

Explore some fun, pretty-in-pink possibilities

Pink Champagne is a very romantic drink and can be very girly. Regular Champagne is made from only three grapes. No, one of them is not the adorable little Champagne grapes seen in the produce section. The three grapes used are Pinot Noir, Pinot Meunier, and Chardonnay. The Pinot Noir and Pinot Meunier are red, and the Chardonnay is white. All grape juice is white/clear. Even inside the red ones, the juice is clear. Only the skins have color. So when making Pink Champagne,

winemakers leave the skins on a little longer to get a pink color, much as they do when making White Zinfandel, Blush, and Rosé wines.

Even though Pink Champagne had been around a long time, not until the 1950s did it explode (no pun intended). The reason was that until that time the color pink hadn't been used in fashion culture. All of a sudden there were pink Cadillacs, pink pumps, pink poodle skirts, pink lipstick, pink

Bubblegum Bubbly

Ingredients

5 ounces banana liqueur
½ ounce peach schnapps
5 ounces brut rose Champagne
Blow pop garnish
Ice

1. Fill a wine glass half with ice.
2. Pour in the ingredients. Add garnish.

Tickled Pink

Ingredients

Pink sugar to rim glass
Organic rose petals
5 ounces raspberry vodka
½ ounce lemon juice
½ ounce rose syrup
5 ounces brut rose Champagne

1. Rim a Champagne glass with pink sugar. Then drop in rose petals.
2. Shake the next three ingredients with ice.
3. Strain into a Champagne glass.
4. Pour in the Champagne.

dresses, and even pink refrigerators and appliances. One icon from the 1950s, Elvis Presley, wore a pink shirt. It has been said that he had the shirt made because, well, quite frankly, there weren't any pink shirts for men at Sears and Roebuck. He was a true fashion trendsetter.

ZOOM

Pink Champagne is seen in the 1957 film *An Affair to Remember* starring Cary Grant and Deborah Kerr. They drink Pink Champagne, then decide it's best not to be together (he's engaged, and she has a boyfriend). Later, arriving separately at the bar, each orders a Pink Champagne cocktail without knowing the other's order until the drinks are on the bar.

Princess for a Day

Ingredients

Edible gold glitter or flake
½ ounce blueberry vodka
1 ounce strawberry-flavored white cranberry juice
5 ounces brut rose Champagne

1. Rim a Champagne glass with edible gold.
2. Pour in the vodka and juice.
3. Pour in the Champagne.

Royal Treatment

You can have fun with the Princess for a Day at special occasion parties. You could provide tiaras or drop very large plastic jewels into the drink (large because you don't want anyone to accidentally swallow one). And on a romantic note, you could drop in a pink diamond engagement ring as part of your proposal.

FRENCH-INSPIRED CHAMPAGNE

Mix up these bubbly concoctions that are based on some fun French icons

The term moulin rouge translates as "red windmill" (hence the red windmill on the building that houses the Parisian cabaret of the same name). Fox Studios gave us an idea of what the Moulin Rouge cabaret is all about when Fox released a film of the same name in 2001. Today the cabaret offers three shows daily. For the evening shows, you have an option to purchase

a show ticket, dinner ticket, or a Champagne ticket. Champagne has always been a staple at the Moulin Rouge since its opening in 1889.

Marie Antoinette was married at age fourteen and became queen at age nineteen in 1770. It is believed that the saucer/coupe style of Champagne glass was created to replicate her

Moulin Rouge

Ingredients

Ice
5 ounces French sweet vermouth
½ ounce sloe gin
5 ounces Champagne
Mini-windmill cherry garnish

1. Fill a wine glass half with ice.
2. Pour in the ingredients. Add garnish.

Marie Antoinette

Ingredients

1 ounce St-Germain elderflower liqueur
5 ounces Champagne
White edible flower garnish

1. Pour liqueur into a coupe Champagne glass.
2. Pour in the Champagne. Add garnish.

breasts. Some people believe this theory because her husband, King Louis XVI, hosted excessive parties at the palace at Versailles. Others say that this theory is not likely because glasses of that shape were not around until the mid-1800s. Nonetheless, it makes a great story.

Bollinger (pronounced bowl-lin-ZHAY) Champagne is dubbed the "James Bond Champagne." It has been featured in nine Bond films to date. Bollinger is one of the very few Champagne houses that is family owned and managed, handed down from generation to generation since 1829.

007

Ingredients

Black sugar to rim glass
1 ounce Blavod black vodka
½ ounce lemon juice
½ ounce simple syrup
3 ounces Bollinger Champagne

1. Rim a Champagne glass with black sugar.
2. Shake the first three ingredients.
3. Strain into the Champagne glass.
4. Pour in Champagne.

Bond Drinking Habits

It's no secret that James Bond and alcohol, well . . . have a bond. To date, believe it or not, Bond has drunk 431 drinks on film. Sixty-five of them are Champagne. Some others include bourbon (57), Scotch (42), Vodka Martini (41), sake (37), brandy and cognac (24), gin (21), red wine (21), white wine (9), Americano (6), Vesper (4), Old Fashioned (4), ouzo (3), Stinger (3), Mint Julep (1), Mojito (1), Negroni (1), Rum Collins (1), and pink gin (1).

SUGAR-FREE CLASSICS
Make classic cocktails that are 100 percent free of sugar

Are you tired of drinking your favorite alcohol with diet cola or plain soda water to avoid the sugar? It doesn't have to be that way. You can make practically every cocktail (and your favorites) without sugar. One trick is to replace the sugar with sugar-free simple syrup. You can learn to make your own in Chapter 19 (Techniques & Recipes). Restaurants and bars seem to only offer diet cola. But when shopping in the soda aisle at your local grocer looking for ideas to bring home . . .

well, your head will spin with the flavor choices.

There are also some great sugar-free syrups on the market. They are available in many flavors so it will open up a world if ideas for you. Let's say for example you like *Blackberry Mojitos*, all you have to do is replace the simple syrup with the sugar free blackberry syrup and voila! Maybe you like *Strawberry Margaritas*? Replace the sugar-free simple syrup again.

Extracts can be found in the spice aisle at your local gro-

Skinny Mojito

Ingredients

Handful of mint leaves
1 ounce lime juice
Ice
1½ ounces light rum
1 ounce sugar-free simple syrup
Soda water
Mint sprig garnish

1. Muddle the mint and lime juice in a tall glass.
2. Fill with cracked or crushed ice.
3. Pour in the next two ingredients, then stir.
4. Top with soda water and stir. Add garnish.

Skinny Margarita

Ingredients

Salt to rim glass (optional)
Ice
1½ ounces tequila
Cap of orange extract
1 ounce lime juice
1 ounce sugar-free simple syrup

1. **Up:** Shake ingredients with ice. Strain into a chilled cocktail glass.
2. **Rocks:** Shake ingredients with ice. Strain into a margarita glass filled with ice.
3. **Frozen:** Blend ingredients with a half cup of ice. Pour into a margarita glass.

cer. Because they don't contain sugar, you can use them to add flavor. The orange extract takes the place of the triple sec that would normally be in the Margarita and Long Island Iced Tea.

MAKE IT EASY

To drink a sugar-free Long Island at the bar is possible. Simply ask the bartender for the triple sec and sweet-and-sour to be omitted and replace the Coke with Diet Coke. For the sour mix, ask for three lemon wedges, two packets of Splenda, and a rocks glass of water. Mix and pour into the drink.

Skinny Long Island Iced Tea

Ingredients

Ice
½ ounce vodka
½ ounce gin
½ ounce rum
½ ounce tequila
Cap of orange extract
1 ounce lemon juice
1 ounce sugar-free simple sugar

Splash of diet cola
Lemon garnish

1. Fill a tall glass with ice.
2. Shake all the ingredients (except the cola) with ice.
3. Strain into the glass.
4. Top with diet cola. Add garnish.

Skinny Whiskey Sour

Ingredients

Ice
1½ ounces whiskey
1 ounce lemon juice
1 ounce sugar-free simple syrup
Orange flag garnish

1. Fill a highball glass with ice.
2. Shake all the ingredients with ice.
3. Strain into the glass. Add garnish.

141

LOW-CARB COCKTAILS
Learn about the wide range of low-carb drink choices

Here are three low-carb cocktails to help springboard some ideas of your own. First know that there are carbohydrates in fruits, vegetables, bread, rice, beans, pasta, grains, and sugar, sugar, sugar. So that leaves proteins. But don't worry, you won't find any steak and egg daiquiris. There is one liquid protein you can incorporate into a cocktail, and it's cream or half-and-half. Of course, the fat content is high because it's an animal product, but it contains zero carbs.

Fruit and vegetable juices sound healthy, and they are, but they are loaded with carbs. And fruit juice is loaded with sugar—natural sugar, but it's still sugar to your body. Any mixer you use for a low-carb cocktail will have to be sugar free. But you're in luck because there are so many choices! There are sugar-free powder mixes and a ton of sugar-free soda flavors. To add an intense citrus flavor, choose Fresca. It has ten flavors to choose from. Another overlooked choice is Diet

Carb-free Alcohol

Your choices for zero/trace-carb alcohol are vodka, gin, rum, tequila, and whiskey. Even the flavored ones are carb free! Yes, alcohol starts as a carb in the beginning (grain, sugar, agave), but the carbs don't carry over in the steam during distillation. Liqueurs, cordials, schnapps, crème, and cream liqueurs are loaded with sugar, so stay away from those.

Skinny Raspberry Lemonade

Ingredients

Ice
¾ ounce raspberry vodka
¾ ounce citrus vodka
6 ounces Crystal Light raspberry lemonade
Lemon and raspberry garnish

1. Fill a tall glass with ice.
2. Shake all the ingredients with ice.
3. Strain into the glass. Add garnish.

Rite. It has an assortment of flavors, too, including tangerine and raspberry. Just walk down the soda aisle at your local grocer, and you'll see possibilities you've never seen before.

Dip rim in the sugar-free syrup first so that cookie crumbs will stick.

· · · · · · · · · YELLOW ● LIGHT · · · · · · · · ·

A lot of flavored soda waters have hit the market recently and can be a little deceiving. Beware if the front label promises, "Fat Free" because all sugar is fat free, but your body converts the sugar into fat. Always make sure you turn the bottle over and read the label if there's sugar in it.

Skinny Chocolate-tini

Ingredients

Ice
2 ounces vanilla vodka
1 ounce Monin sugar-free chocolate syrup
2 ounces half-and-half
Crushed sugar-free Oreo to rim glass

1. Rim a cocktail glass with crushed sugar-free Oreos.
2. Shake all the ingredients with ice.
3. Strain into the glass.

Skinny Pirate

Ingredients

Ice
1½ ounces Captain Morgan spiced rum
5 ounces diet cola

1. Fill a highball glass with ice.
2. Pour in the ingredients.

HEALTHY & GREEN DRINKS

ORGANIC VODKA & GIN DRINKS
Drinking green is easy when you have many organic spirit and mixer choices

Rain is organic vodka that was ahead of its time. It hit the market in 1996 when people were walking around with pagers in their pockets and never dreamed they'd have a computer at home. Rain is made in small batches from 100 percent organic white corn in Kentucky. The packaging is made from 100 percent recyclable materials, and for every purchase the

company donates money to the Wilderness Society. It has won several gold awards.

Other organic vodkas include Square One vodka (2006). It's made from North Dakota organic rye and Teton Mountain water. The company gives after-tax profits to land and water environmental causes. 360 Vodka (2007) has an 85 percent

Mary Me

Ingredients

Filtered ice
1½ ounces organic vodka
5 ounces organic Bloody Mary mix
Variety of organic garnishes

1. Fill a tall glass with filtered ice.
2. Pour in the organic vodka and organic Bloody Mary mix. Stir.
3. Add organic garnish.

Day at the Spa

Ingredients

1 ounce organic lemon juice
½ organic cucumber peeled and sliced
3 sprigs organic mint leaves
Filtered ice
2 ounces Rain Organic's vodka
1 ounce organic honey syrup
4 ounces organic ginger soda
Mint sprig garnish

1. Muddle the first three ingredients in a tall glass.
2. Add filtered cracked or crushed ice.
3. Add the last three ingredients and stir. Top with garnish.

144

recycled glass bottle, and the company uses eco-friendly packaging. Ocean Vodka (2007) is made in Maui with MaHa-Lo Hawaii Deep Sea Water and organic grains. The company donates to organizations working to conserve the world's ocean resources. Vodka 14 (2007) is made in Colorado with Rocky Mountain spring water and organic grain. Bluecoat American dry gin (2006) uses organic grains and herbs. It's made in Philadelphia. Q Tonic water is made with handpicked quinine from the Peruvian Andes. It uses organic agave as the sweetener.

Liquid Herb Garden

Ingredients

Filtered ice
1½ ounces gin
1 ounce lavender organic simple syrup
½ ounce organic lime juice
½ ounce organic lemon juice
4 ounces organic Q Tonic
Organic mint sprig and sprinkle of dried lavender garnish

1. Fill a tall glass with filtered ice.
2. Add the first four ingredients and stir.
3. Top with organic Q Tonic. Add organic garnish.

Juniper Treehugger

Ingredients

Filtered ice
1½ ounces American Bluecoat organic gin
1 ounce organic maple simple syrup
½ ounce organic lime juice
½ ounce organic lemon juice
2 dashes orange bitters

2 ounces filtered charged water or organic soda water

1. Fill a tall glass with filtered ice.
2. Shake the first five ingredients with filtered ice.
3. Strain into the glass.
4. Top with filtered charged water.

145

ORGANIC RUM & TEQUILA DRINKS

The tropics give a green light to eco-drinking set in a tropical paradise

A few organically produced rums are on the market: Papagayo Organic spiced rum (from Paraguay), Matraga white rum (from southern Brazil), Utkins Fairtrade white rum (Paraguay), and Rivers Royal (Grenada). As for tequila, look for 4 Copas Tequila. No pesticides or chemicals are used in farming the agave plants, and the maker uses only organic yeast in fermentation.

Don't forget that you can infuse organic spirits with organic products. For example, for the Fresh Funky Monkey, you could make infused banana rum. Or make chocolate rum. Vanilla rum would be yummy, too, by using organic vanilla pods. Also available is organic chocolate soy milk.

For the Blueberry Eco-Mojito, you could make infused mint

Fresh Funky Monkey

Ingredients

2 ounces organic chocolate syrup
Filtered ice
2 ounces organic rum
1 organic banana
3 ounces organic soy milk
Organic shaved chocolate garnish

1. Squirt 1 ounce of the organic chocolate syrup into half a tall glass.
2. Pour the rest of the ingredients into a blender with a cup of ice and blend.
3. Pour into the glass. Add garnish

Blueberry Eco-Mojito

Ingredients

Handful of organic mint leaves
Handful of organic blueberries
1 ounce lime juice
Ice
1½ ounces organic rum
1 ounce organic raw simple syrup
Filtered charged water or organic soda water

Organic blueberry and mint garnish

1. Muddle mint, blueberries, and lime juice in a tall glass.
2. Fill with cracked or crushed ice.
3. Pour in the next two ingredients, then stir.
4. Top with filtered charged water. Add garnish.

rum. If you don't care for blueberries, then simply replace them with another favorite fruit such as organic strawberries, blackberries, peaches, or black cherries. It's all up to you!

The Natural SeñoRita is basically an organic margarita with organic orange juice used to substitute the orange liqueur. You can also use other organic juices in its place. Pomegranate would be nice. Other substitutions include Monin organic raspberry syrup, organic fruits, purees, or organic jams and jellies. While you're at it, you can infuse the tequila with many flavors, too!

······· GREEN ● LIGHT ·······

Investing in a soda siphon will enable you to make freshly charged water. You've seen such siphons in the old movies where people walk up to the home bar and squirt soda water into their drink. Even green bars across America are using them. Simply fill with filtered water. You can also make fresh whipped cream this way.

Natural SeñoRita

Ingredients

Ice
1½ ounces organic tequila
1 ounce organic orange juice
1 oz organic lime juice
1 ounce organic raw simple syrup
Optional organic sea salt rim and lime garnish

1. Up: Shake ingredients with ice. Strain into a chilled cocktail glass.
2. Rocks: Shake ingredients with ice. Strain into a margarita glass filled with ice.
3. Frozen: Blend ingredients with a half cup of ice. Pour into a margarita glass.

Organic Sea Salt

Salt is a mineral, not a plant, so it can't be referred to as "organically grown." However, it can be classified as "certified organic." The seawater must be inspected to pass certification, and strict guidelines must be met. For example, production must be only by hand, evaporation can be only through sun and wind, and natural circulation must occur.

ORGANIC WHISKEY & BRANDY DRINKS

Pour, shake, and stir up some classic spinoffs with a green influence

Whiskeys and brandies are coming up behind in the organic race, but it's not because they aren't making an effort. There is more involved in these spirits. For starters, they are aged. Vodka, gin, rum, and tequila can de distilled and poured straight into the bottle. Not whiskey, brandy, and cognacs.

So far the United States,, Canada, and Ireland haven't produced any organic whiskey, but Scotland has! Its first one is called "Benromach" and is *certified organic* by the Soil Associa-

tion. So, in every step the company meets Soil Association guidelines to be able to put those two words on its label. As for the casks used for aging, the company imports American virgin oak casts made of wood that is harvested from environmentally managed forests. Two more Scotches are Highland Harvest and Da Mihle. As for organic brandy and cognac, there are L&L, Guy Pinard, and Lafragette.

If you're not able to find any of these organic whiskeys and

Alexander Notes

For the Dandy Brandy Alexander, you can use other organic chocolate syrups found at Whole Foods, but first try the coffee aisle and look for the syrup there. It will have the same consistency of the commercial syrups. You could also substitute the chocolate and soy milk with organic chocolate soy milk. And look for an organic stick of nutmeg to grate.

Bee Natural

Ingredients

2 ounces organic single-malt Scotch whisky
1 ounce organic raw honey syrup
Filtered ice
Organic lemon twist garnish

1. Pour the ingredients into a rocks glass and stir until honey is dissolved.
2. Add filtered ice. Add garnish.

brandies, don't worry. Focus on the organics of the mixers because you have a few decisions to make. For example, for the Bee Natural, the organic lemon is a no-brainer, but there will be a large assortment of organic honeys to choose from.

Radical Raspberry Sidecar

Ingredients

Raw organic sugar to rim glass
Filtered ice
2 ounces organic cognac
½ ounce Monin organic raspberry syrup (or from scratch)
1 ounce organic lemon juice

1. Rim a cocktail glass with organic raw sugar.
2. Shake all the ingredients with filtered ice.
3. Strain into the glass.

Dandy Brandy Alexander

Ingredients

Filtered ice
2 ounces organic cognac or brandy
1 ounce organic chocolate syrup
2 ounces organic soy milk
Organic nutmeg sprinkle garnish

1. Chill a cocktail glass with filtered ice.
2. Shake all the ingredients with filtered ice.
3. Strain into the glass. Add garnish.

ANTIOXIDANT DRINKS
These drinks are actually good for your heart and many of your other body parts

What is so great about antioxidants? Well, antioxidants are found in all fruits, vegetables, and things grown in the earth. Some are just richer in antioxidants than others. When antioxidants enter our body, they act like little doctors, running around repairing damage from the free radicals that have entered our body. Free radicals come from pesticides, pollution, cigarette smoke, and

all the other things that aren't meant to enter our body. Doctors have long lists of the benefits of antioxidants. A few benefits include improved immune system, better vision, liver cleansing, cancer prevention, and lower blood pressure.

Some ingredients on this page probably are new to you. So, let's briefly go over some of them. Kefir is a cultured, enzyme-

Mean Green Tea

Ingredients

Filtered ice
2 ounces organic vodka
1 ounce organic raw honey syrup
2 ounces organic lemon juice
2 ounces organic green tea
1 teaspoon Spirulina powder (or ½ ounce wheat grass juice)
5 drops GSE

3 ounces Blue Sky organic ginger ale
Organic lemon garnish

1. Fill a tall glass with filtered ice.
2. Shake the next six ingredients with filtered ice.
3. Strain into the glass.
4. Top with organic ginger ale. Add garnish.

Down the Rabbit Hole

Ingredients

Filtered ice
2 ounces organic vodka
2 ounces organic carrot juice
1 ounce pomegranate juice
1 ounce organic raw honey
4 ounces organic yogurt
2 ounces kefir
Handful of organic blueberries

Organic carrot stick and blueberries garnish

1. Blend ingredients with a cup of filtered ice. Add additional ice if needed.
2. Taste to determine sweetness. If preferred sweeter, simply add more honey.
3. Pour into a stemmed glass. Add garnish.

rich food filled with friendly microorganisms that help balance your inner ecosystem. It's actually more nutritious than yogurt.

GSE (grapefruit seed extract) is a highly concentrated liquid made from the seeds of grapefruit. It has a multitude of uses. First know that it should always be diluted with water and should not come in full-strength contact with your skin. You can gargle with it, purify water with it, or clean anything with it (hospitals use it in the operating room).

Spirulina comes from blue-green algae and contains many disease-preventive nutrients.

ZOOM

Many foods have antioxidant properties. Here are some juices at the top of the list that you can mix into a cocktail: blueberry, pomegranate, blackberry, raspberry, strawberry, cranberry (not bottled), Granny Smith apple, prune, plum, black cherry, red grape, carrot, wheat grass, and açaí. Other liquids include soy milk, kefir, green tea, white tea, aloe, GSE, and red wine.

Fountain of Youth

Ingredients

Filtered ice
2 ounces organic black cherry-infused organic vodka
1 ounce açaí juice
½ ounce aloe juice
1 ounce POM Wonderful cherry juice
1 ounce organic lemon juice
3 ounces organic sparkling pear cider
Organic cherry garnish

1. Shake all the ingredients (except the organic pear cider) with filtered ice.
2. Strain into a large stemmed glass.
3. Top with organic pear cider. Add garnish.

Youth Juice

Açaí (pronounced ah-SIGH-ee) berry juice is the latest antioxidant phenomenon. It is found on palm trees along the Amazon River and, as you guessed, contains ingredients to cure whatever ails you. However, most intriguing are studies that show a slowing of the aging process. So açaí berry juice wins the title of best fountain of youth juice.

151

VALENTINE DRINKS

Shake up some love potions for the most romantic day of the year

Whether you're planning an intimate evening with someone you love or getting together with friends you love, these love potions will melt your beating heart.

The Kama Sutra is made with cherry vodka, but that can easily be replaced with raspberry or strawberry vodka if that suits your taste buds. The most important ingredient is the lemon juice because you need the citrus to balance out the sweetness of the sugar rim. The Alizé is available in two fla-

vors and colors; make sure you get the red passion flavor.

To notch up the fun with the Pucker Up, why not lipstick kiss the outside of the glass? Red-waxed lips can be found in most candy stores in most malls. You can also drop in a few conversation hearts!

Valentine's Day is one of the American holidays brought over from the Old World. England's King Henry VIII declared it a holiday in 1537, and today six countries officially list it

Kama Sutra

Pucker Up

Ingredients

Sugar to rim glass
Ice
1 ounce cherry vodka
1 ounce Alizé Red Passion liqueur
1 ounce fresh lemon juice
2 ounces Smirnoff Ice
Cherry garnish

1. Rim a cocktail glass with sugar.
2. Shake the first three ingredients with ice.
3. Strain into the glass.
4. Top with Smirnoff Ice. Add garnish.

Ingredients

Ice
1 ounce sour apple vodka
1 ounce watermelon pucker schnapps
1 ounce lime juice
Wax lips garnish

1. Chill a cocktail glass with ice.
2. Shake the ingredients with ice.
3. Strain into the glass. Add garnish.

on their calendars. That makes you wonder why it took over three hundred years for someone to invent the first Valentine's Day box of chocolates. Richard Cadbury introduced it in 1868. So, why not put that box of chocolates to use and garnish a Valentine cocktail?

ZOOM

Do you love those little candy hearts called "conversation hearts"? They were first marketed in 1866 but were called "motto hearts." The name changed sometime at the beginning of the twentieth century. It has been reported that eight billion of these hearts are sold between January 1 and February 14. Today you can even special order them with words of your choice.

Box of Chocolates

Ingredients

Chocolate swirl
Ice
1 ounce vanilla vodka
1 ounce butterscotch schnapps
1 ounce Irish cream
1 ounce half-and-half
Chocolate candy garnish

1. Swirl chocolate into cocktail glass.
2. Shake the ingredients with ice.
3. Strain into the glass. Add garnish.

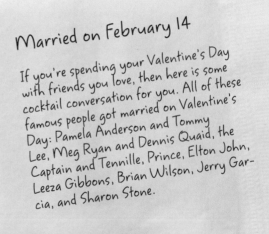

Married on February 14

If you're spending your Valentine's Day with friends you love, then here is some cocktail conversation for you. All of these famous people got married on Valentine's Day: Pamela Anderson and Tommy Lee, Meg Ryan and Dennis Quaid, the Captain and Tennille, Prince, Elton John, Leeza Gibbons, Brian Wilson, Jerry Garcia, and Sharon Stone.

HOLIDAY DRINKS

ST. PATRICK'S DRINKS
May the road (and these Irish drinks) rise up to meet you

A bar in San Francisco claims to make two thousand Irish coffees a day. It's true! The bar is the Buena Vista Café, and it's been sitting at Hyde and Beach Street since the early 1900s. So how did Irish Coffee become famous in California when it's an Irish drink? Oh, that starts at the Shannon airport in Dublin. See, in 1952, Jack Koeppler (owner of the Buena Vista) was told about the coffee from a travel writer who frequented his bar. Jack wanted to duplicate the recipe, so they both tried many times but failed. So, Jack flew to Ireland on the wings of intention to get the real recipe for Irish Coffee. He succeeded, and the rest is history. The recipe on this page is the same recipe at the Buena Vista Café.

A St. Patty drink would not be complete if it wasn't green, so the Sweet Clover fits the bill. The recipe leans more toward what an Irish beauty's taste buds might welcome, so if you need to twist it up to be more of a manly Irish laddie drink,

Irish Toasts

Drinking Irish would not be complete without a traditional Irish toast, so here are three: May you live as long as you want and never want as long as you live; may your home always be too small to hold all your friends; here's to being single, drinking doubles, and seeing triple!

Irish Coffee

Ingredients

1½ ounces Irish whiskey
3 sugar cubes
5 ounces fresh brewed strong black coffee
Hand-whipped cream garnish

1. Preheat an Irish coffee glass.
2. Pour in the ingredients. Stir.
3. Garnish with hand-whipped cream poured over a spoon. Do not stir.

then pour all the ingredients into a tall glass of ice and add an extra ounce of whiskey.

The magically delicious Lucky Charms cereal with a leprechaun as a mascot was created in 1963. Ironically, it's not available in Ireland. The first lucky marshmallows were pink hearts, yellow moons, orange stars, and green clovers. Others include blue diamonds (1975), purple horseshoes (1984), red balloons (1989), rainbows (1992), pots of gold (1994), leprechaun hats (1996), shooting stars (1998), and yellow hourglasses (2008).

Even the festive color matches the holiday spirit.

Sweet Clover

Ingredients

Ice
1½ ounces Irish whiskey
1 ounce melon liqueur
1 ounce lemon juice
½ ounce simple syrup
Washed and rinsed clovers for garnish

1. Chill a cocktail glass with ice.
2. Shake the ingredients with ice.
3. Strain into the glass. Add garnish

Lucky Charms-tini

Ingredients

Ice
1½ ounces blueberry vodka
2 ounces strawberry milk
Handful of Lucky Charms cereal garnish

1. Chill a coupe-style glass with ice.
2. Shake the ingredients with ice.
3. Strain into the glass. Add garnish.

SUMMER & JULY FOURTH DRINKS

Keep your cool by making some refreshing drinks for celebrating or just kicking back

To beat the heat, summer drinks should be mouth watering, light, refreshing, bubbly, and, above all else, cold. The season allows a wide assortment of fruits to be used, so your imagination can go wild, especially when you have so many fruity flavored spirits to choose from as well.

Let's take the Watermelon Kiwi Cooler. In cocktail terminol-

ogy a cooler is wine with lemon-lime soda (or sweetened carbonation). So, this opens up a whole world of possibilities. You can use different wines, but make sure you stick with dry ones because you need to balance the sweetness of the soda you're adding. And if you need help finding what is available as a replacement for the lemon-lime soda, then

Happy Birthday, America

For the Independence Colada, you can pour the blue color on the bottom and the red on top if you prefer. Red and blue fruits like blueberries, raspberries, strawberries, and blackberries can be incorporated as well. And, of course, the ultimate is to serve the drink with a lit sparkler. Make sure to take precautions if you do.

Independence Colada

Ingredients

½ ounce grenadine
Ice
1½ ounces light rum
4 ounces piña colada mix
½ ounce blue Curacao

1. Pour the grenadine into the bottom of a tropical glass.
2. Blend the rum and piña colada mix with a cup of ice.
3. Pour into the glass.
4. Float the blue Curacao on top.

just take a walk down the soda aisle at your local grocer. You can also choose sugar-free varieties. And you can add liqueurs and flavored spirits. But keep their portions on the low side because you already have 4 ounces of wine in the cooler to begin with. Other garnishes you can try are grapes, cantaloupe balls, nectarines, all berries, cherries, cubed pear, cubed mango, cubed pineapple, star fruit, star anise, edible flowers, or citrus. It's really all up to you.

Provide picks to make it easier to eat the garnish.

Watermelon Kiwi Cooler

Ingredients

Ice
4 ounces dry white wine
1 ounce lemon juice
4 ounces lemon-lime soda of choice
Watermelon balls and kiwi slices garnish

1. Fill a wine glass half with ice.
2. Add all the ingredients and stir. Add garnish.
3. You can substitute the lemon-lime soda for sugar-free lemon-lime soda.

Strawberry Pom Lemonade

Ingredients

Ice
1½ ounces strawberry vodka
1 ounce pomegranate juice
½ ounce handmade lemonade
Lemon and strawberry garnish

1. Fill a tall glass with ice.
2. Shake all the ingredients with ice.
3. Strain into the glass. Add garnish.

HALLOWEEN DRINKS

Scare up some haunting and spooky drinks to get everyone in the spirit

Blavod black vodka is without a doubt the best Halloween spirit on the planet. It's the only black vodka in the world and has a multitude of uses in creating cocktail fun. The black-as–a-witch's-hat color comes from catechu, which is extracted from the bark of sacred acacia trees found in India and elsewhere in southern Asia. Through the centuries, catechu has been used in medicine to cure colds, coughs, diarrhea, and fevers and boiled in water to add to baths to ease pain. It can be used as an astringent, breath freshener, and body disinfectant. Commercially it's used for tanning, dyeing, preserving, and printing. And in modern times it's best used for spooky-licious Halloween drinks. It tastes exactly like regular vodka, so

Devil's Blood

Ingredients

Red sugar to rim
Ice
4 ounces cranberry juice
1½ ounces black vodka

1. Rim a highball glass with red sugar, then fill with ice.
2. Pour in the cranberry juice.
3. Carefully layer the vodka over a spoon on top of the juice.

Rotten Pumpkin

Ingredients

Ice
4 ounces orange juice
1½ ounces black vodka
Black sugar-dipped orange garnish

1. Fill a highball glass with ice.
2. Pour in the orange juice.
3. Carefully layer the vodka over a spoon on top of the juice.

there's no need to be afraid of the dark!

Also, don't be afraid to treat yourself and your friends to some tricks! You can give the black vodka extra flavor by infusing it with a favorite flavor. This will open up a casket of possibilities. Also, why not drop in some lighted ice cubes? Glow sticks would be awesome in the ghost aura or any of these Halloween drinks. Wrapping them on the outside of the glass is a great option, too.

Ghost Aura

Ingredients

Ice
Shredded coconut to rim glass
1½ ounces coconut rum
½ ounce melon liqueur
5 ounces lemon-lime soda

1. Rim a tall glass with shredded coconut, then fill with ice.
2. Pour the first two ingredients into the glass. Stir.
3. Top with lemon-lime soda.

Berry Scary-tini

Ingredients

Black sugar to rim glass
Ice
¾ ounce black vodka
¾ ounce blueberry vodka
1 ounce raspberry liqueur
2 ounces lemon juice
Raspberry garnish

1. Rim a cocktail glass with black sugar.
2. Shake all the ingredients with ice.
3. Strain into the glass. Add garnish

HOLIDAY DRINKS

THANKSGIVING DRINKS

You'll have a lot to be thankful for after tasting these seasonal libations

The Honey Baked Turkey is a festive holiday spin from the ordinary, any-night cocktail nicknamed the "Cosmo." This award-winning Wild Turkey Honey Liqueur is made with honey, citrus, vanilla, and, of course, bourbon. It's also 71 proof. If you happen to discover that you forgot the cranberry sauce but not the cranberry juice, then start shaking it up, pilgrim!

The Hot Apple Pie is simple to make after the apple cider is warmed. It's absolutely perfect for an after-Thanksgiving toddy. The Tuaca makes all the difference. The Italian liqueur is sweet with vanilla, citrus, and spices. It is a perfect combination with the warm apple cider. If some family member has cranked the heat up, or you live in a warm climate and

Honey Baked Turkey

Ingredients

Ice
2 ounces Wild Turkey Honey Liqueur
1 ounce lemon juice
1 ounce cranberry juice

1. Chill a cocktail glass with ice.
2. Shake all the ingredients with ice.
3. Strain into the glass.

Hot Apple Pie

Ingredients

1½ ounces Tuaca
5 ounces hot apple cider
Whipped cream garnish

1. Preheat a mug with hot water or set it in the microwave for 30 seconds.
2. Pour in the ingredients. Add garnish.

crave something chilly and light slipping down your throat, then shake it up with ice, apple juice, and lemon juice. It's equally as yummy.

Because Thanksgiving is about family and friends getting together, Blackberry Plum Wine is a warm and welcoming choice to offer arriving guests. It's perfect to make ahead of time and an easy recipe to multiply to suit your guest list. The best thing is that you can shop for a less expensive red wine to help save a few bucks.

Blackberry Plum Wine

Ingredients

1 750-milliliter bottle red wine
3 plums, sliced
½ pint blackberries
1 teaspoon nutmeg
½ cup sugar

1. Heat the first three ingredients in a pot to a simmer. Stir gently.
2. Add the last two ingredients and simmer for 5 minutes. Stir gently.
3. Take off stove. Allow infusing for at least 20 minutes before serving.
Yields four 6-ounce servings

Self-Service Holiday

The Hot Apple Pie and Blackberry Plum Wine are perfect candidates to set up for self-service. Simply designate a place on a table, bar, or similar furniture piece in your house. Both drinks can sit warm and ready in a crock pot on the lowest setting. Provide a ladle, cups, and napkins, and you're set.

HOLIDAY DRINKS

Get into the spirit of the season with some holiday-inspired libations

December is the exception to other holidays during the rest of the year because the whole month is dedicated to celebration. So you need choices of drinks that vary in flavor and color.

If you like coconut, chocolate, and vanilla, then the ice blue *Winter Wonderland* is the perfect holiday choice for you. To make the coconut-vanilla snowballs ahead of time, gather these items: two cookie pans, vanilla ice cream, shredded

white coconut, and rubber gloves. Place one cookie pan in the freezer, then pour the coconut onto the other pan. In assembly-line fashion, put on the gloves, scoop some ice cream, form it into a ball, then roll in the coconut. Place on the tray in the freezer and keep working like a North Pole elf until you make the amount of snowballs needed.

Dark rum is made with molasses, and when mixed with eggnog it creates a taste much deeper and richer than that

Winter Wonderland

Ingredients

Ice
2 ounces coconut rum
1 ounce white crème de cacao
Dash blue Curacao
Coconut vanilla ice cream ball garnish

1. Chill a cocktail glass with ice.
2. Shake all the ingredients with ice.
3. Strain into the glass. Add garnish.

Molasses Eggnog

Ingredients

Ice
1½ ounces chilled dark rum
5 ounces chilled eggnog
Nutmeg garnish

1. Chill a mug with ice.
2. Pour in the chilled ingredients. Add garnish.

of plain light rum or brandy. Aged and amber rums will work well with eggnog, and some people love spiced rum in eggnog. It also tastes better if both the rum and eggnog start cold, so keep both in the fridge until ready.

Candy Cane

Ingredients

Crushed candy cane to rim glass
Ice
2 ounces vanilla vodka
1 ounce peppermint schnapps or white crème de menthe

1. Rim a cocktail glass with crushed peppermint candy.
2. Shake all the ingredients with ice.
3. Strain into the glass.

Mr. Grinch Juice

Ingredients

Red sugar to rim glass
Ice
1 ounce sour apple vodka
1 ounce sour apple schnapps
2 ounces lime juice

1. Rim a cocktail glass with red sugar.
2. Shake all the ingredients with ice.
3. Strain into the glass.

HOLIDAY DRINKS

TRADITIONAL SANGRIA
Learn to create some traditional sangrias to help you grasp the basics

Sangria in its basic form is just wine, fruit, juices, and spirit mixed together and topped with something bubbly. Although no one knows when the first sangria was made, it's believed to be a longtime social drink that came from Spain. A Spanish housewife probably needed to make a batch for a festive evening with friends, then looked at her pantry inventory and *voilá!* (excuse the French), sangria was born.

The ideal way to prepare sangria is to allow most of the fruits to sit overnight in the fridge to soak up the alcohol and flavor, but you can cheat and make it a few hours ahead as well. Fruits used mostly as decoration such as star fruit, for example, can be added right before serving.

KNACK BARTENDING BASICS

Spanish Sangria

Ingredients
1 750-milliliter bottle rioja
½ cup Spanish brandy
1 cup orange juice
½ cup lemon juice
¼ cup sugar or simple syrup
Orange slices
2 oranges, 2 lemons for garnish
Ice
24 ounces soda water
Yields 8 servings

1. Pour the first five ingredients into a pitcher or large container. Stir.
2. Add orange slices and let sit in the fridge for 3–12 hours.
3. When ready pour about 6 ounces of sangria into fruit-garnished wine glasses half filled with ice.
4. Top each glass with 3 ounces soda water.

Italian Sangria

Ingredients
1 750-milliliter bottle Italian red wine
½ cup grappa
1 cup orange juice
½ cup lemon juice
¼ cup sugar or simple syrup
Orange and peach slices
2 oranges, 2 lemons for garnish
24 ounces soda water
Ice

Yields 8 servings

1. Pour first five ingredients into a pitcher. Stir.
2. Add orange, peach slices; let sit in fridge 3–12 hours.
3. When ready pour 6 ounces sangria into fruit-garnished wine glasses half filled with ice.
4. Top each glass with 3 ounces soda water.

The traditional red wine used in Spain for sangrias is rioja. These traditional sangrias have ingredients that pertain to their country. Feel free to use other typical ingredients from their countries as well.

The desired overall taste of sangria is slightly sweet. Different wines have different sweetness levels, but don't fret. If the sangria is too sour, then add more sweetener, and if it's too sweet, then add a sour with more citrus juice.

French Sangria

Ingredients
1 750-milliliter bottle French red wine
½ cup Grand Marnier
1 cup orange juice
½ cup lemon juice
¼ cup sugar or simple syrup
Orange slices
2 oranges, 2 lemons, and ½ pint raspberries
24 ounces soda water

Ice
Yields 8 servings

1. Pour first five ingredients into pitcher. Stir. Add slices; let sit in fridge 3–12 hours.
2. When ready pour 6 ounces sangria into fruit-garnished wine glasses half filled with ice.
3. Top each glass with 3 ounces soda water.

Sangria Tips

- Less expensive wine works fine.

- Go seasonal with the fruit.

- Serve over ice in garnished wine glasses.

- Explore the many choices of carbonation available.

- Try serving with bamboo skewers so that the fruit can be speared and eaten by your guests.

RED SANGRIA
Experiment with new flavors to mix for your next mixer of friends

Now that you know the basics of sangria, you can branch out of the traditional and think of ideas on your own. First, determine what you have in your own fridge and cabinets, then make a list of what you need.

Practically any liquor, liqueur, juice, spice, fruit, or carbonation is possible. As for spirits, you can use brandy, vodka, rum, gin, tequila, and whiskey in flavors available. Liqueur choices abound, and juices can also be replaced with nectars and purees. More flavor combinations to try include kiwi-strawberry, mango-vanilla, spiced pear, pineapple-ginger, raspberry-lychee, tangerine-clove, apple-Amaretto, and chili-lime.

To add a zing for your guests, you can also get creative by freezing fun edibles in ice cubes. For the recipes given, you could make ice cubes with cherries, berries, pomegranate seeds or chopped apples, and lemons. Simply drop your ed-

Chocolate Cherry Sangria

Ingredients
1 750-milliliter bottle red wine
½ cup cherry brandy
½ cup white crème de cacao
½ cup lemon juice
1 cup maraschino or fresh cherries
Ice
24 ounces black cherry soda
Yields 8 servings

1. Pour the first four ingredients into a pitcher. Stir.
2. Add cherries and juice.
3. When ready pour about 6 ounces of sangria into fruit-garnished wine glasses half filled with ice.
4. Top each glass with 3 ounces black cherry soda.

Blackberry Apple Maple Sangria

Ingredients
1 750-milliliter bottle red wine
½ cup blackberry brandy
½ cup apple juice or cider
½ cup lemon juice
¼ cup maple syrup
1 pint blackberries, 2 red apples, and 2 lemons
Ice
24 ounces lemon-lime soda
Yields 8 servings

1. Pour the first five ingredients into a pitcher. Stir.
2. Add blackberries and apples.
3. When ready pour 6 ounces sangria into fruit-garnished wine glasses half filled with ice.
4. Top each glass with 3 ounces lemon-lime soda.

ible choice into the cavities of the ice trays, then fill with water and freeze. Continue the process over a number of days until you collect a nice big bowl of them in the freezer. That is, unless you have a large freezer and many trays to freeze at one time.

At the 1964 World's Fair in New York, Spain spent $7 million to build a romantic Spanish courtyard filled with Spanish art, music, flowers, and fine dining. The air was filled with flamenco music as visitors strolled through the winding courtyard holding glasses of sangria. That just happened to be when the U.S. was introduced to red wine punch (sangria).

For all sangrias, add fruit after initial ingredients & then let sit in the fridge 3-12 hours before serving.

Raspberry Pom Peach Sangria

Ingredients
1 750-milliliter bottle red wine
½ cup peach schnapps
½ cup pomegranate juice
½ cup lemon juice
24 ounces raspberry-flavored soda
2 peaches, 2 lemons, and ½ pint raspberries
Ice
Yields 8 servings

1. Pour the first four ingredients into a pitcher. Stir.
2. Add peaches.
3. When ready pour 6 ounces sangria into fruit-garnished wine glasses half filled with ice.
4. Top each glass with 3 ounces raspberry-flavored soda.

Red Chai Sangria

Ingredients
1 750-milliliter bottle red wine
½ cup Tuaca
½ cup apple juice or cider
½ cup lemon juice
2 red apples
Teaspoon of ground cinnamon
Medium bag of cinnamon red hot candy
Ice
24 ounces cream soda

Yields 8 servings

1. Pour the first four ingredients into a pitcher. Stir.
2. Add apples.
3. When ready pour 6 ounces sangria into cinnamon red hot-garnished wine glasses half filled with ice.
4. Top each glass with 3 ounces cream soda.

THEME RED SANGRIA

Have vino-licious fun by stirring up some theme sangria for your friends

Without a doubt, sangria is a libation meant to be shared with friends and family. There's no reason why you can't create a big pitcher or bowl to match a theme.

For a fiesta theme, go crazy with lots of colorful fruit as if you were stuffing a piñata. This would be great sangria for a Cinco de Mayo party, too! The spirit used for Fiesta Sangria is

tequila. You can replace it with flavored tequila if you prefer. Agave syrup is also called "agave nectar" and is made from the agave plant (which is the plant that tequila is made from). You can find it at Whole Foods.

The Midnight at the Oasis Sangria would be wonderful to serve at an Arabian or desert theme party. You could even

Fiesta Sangria

Ingredients

1 750-milliliter bottle red wine
½ cup tequila
½ cup pineapple juice
½ cup orange juice
½ cup lime juice
¼ cup agave syrup
An assortment of colorful fruits
Ice
24 ounces lemon-lime soda

Yields 8 servings
1. Pour first six ingredients into a pitcher. Stir.
2. Add an assortment of fruit.
3. When ready pour 6 ounces sangria into fruit-garnished wine glasses half filled with ice.
4. Top each glass with 3 ounces lemon-lime soda.

Passionate Summer Holiday Sangria

Ingredients

1 750-milliliter bottle red wine
½ cup Alizé Red Passion liqueur
½ cup pineapple juice
½ cup lemon juice
¼ cup honey syrup
1 pint strawberries and 1 cup seedless grapes
Ice
24 ounces pink Champagne

Yields 8 servings

1. Pour first five ingredients into a pitcher. Stir.
2. Add some of the fruit.
3. When ready pour 6 ounces sangria into fruit-garnished wine glasses half filled with ice.
4. Top each glass with 3 ounces pink Champagne.

whip up some for a midnight pool party! The name comes from the romantic song of the same title, and the song is filled with camels, cactus, belly dancers, harems, sultans, palm trees, a half moon, and, of course, an oasis. Star fruit can represent the stars in the midnight sky, half oranges = half moons, raw sugar = sand, and pineapple fronds = palm trees. This romantic sangria works for a romantic party of two.

Midnight at the Oasis Sangria

Ingredients
1 750-milliliter bottle red wine
½ cup pineapple vodka
½ cup tangerine juice
½ cup lemon juice
¼ cup raw sugar or raw sugar simple syrup
2 oranges, 1 cup pineapple fronds, pineapple, and 1 star fruit
Ice

24 ounces lemon-lime soda
Yields 8 servings

1. Pour first five ingredients into a pitcher. Stir.
2. Add oranges and pineapple.
3. When ready pour 6 ounces sangria into fruit-garnished wine glasses half filled with ice.
4. Top each glass with 3 ounces lemon-lime soda.

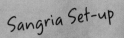

Sangria Set-up

When having guests over, it's best to designate a drink area that can be accessed from all four sides to encourage mingling and conversation. Always have this area decorated to match your theme and stocked with everything a guest may need. Ice scoops and a trash can may sound minor, but they are tools that will be used.

SANGRIAS

WHITE SANGRIA
Reach for a golden bottle of wine to make a lighter, yet still refreshing sangria

If you like traditional red sangria, then you will love the white version! Some people prefer it because it has a translucency that allows the beautiful fruit to shine through. White sangria is also known as "Sangria Blanco," and the best wine to use for a Sangria Blanco is a dry wine like Sauvignon Blanc. This way the dryness of the wine will balance with the sweetness

added to it. If you use a sweeter white wine like a Riesling or Chardonnay, then balance the sweetness by adding more lemon or lime juice and omitting the sugar.

The pear brandy in the White Pear-adise Sangria can be substituted with pear schnapps or pear vodka. And if you don't care for honey, then replace it with a sweetener of your

Translucent Mixer

The classic white sangria is made with apple juice because apple juice was the only translucent sweet juice for a long time. Today we have white grape and white cranberry juice as great choices. Lemon and lime juices are still great for the sour needed to balance the sweetness in a white sangria, and clear spirit and liqueur choices are plentiful.

Classic White Sangria

Ingredients
1 cup apple juice
½ cup lemon juice
1 cup water
¼ cup sugar or simple syrup
2 cinnamon sticks
1 750-milliliter bottle cava white wine
2 oranges, 2 red apples, 2 lemons sliced
Ice

24 ounces soda water
Yields 8 servings

1. Slowly heat juices, water, sugar, sticks 15 minutes. Add wine, fruit; stir. Chill 3–12 hours.
2. When ready pour 6 ounces sangria into fruit-garnished wine glasses half filled with ice.
3. Top each glass with 3 ounces soda water.

choice. Other flavors that would work well in this sangria include ginger liqueur, ginger ale, elderflower liqueur, peach, and violet. Keep in mind that a violet liqueur or syrup would change the color of the sangria to a light purple. This may or may not be something that interests you.

The White Granny Smith Mint Sangria can use sour apple schnapps in place of the sugar for a more intense green apple taste. The color, of course, will change as well.

White Pear-adise Sangria

Ingredients
1 750-milliliter bottle dry white wine
½ cup pear brandy
½ cup white grape juice
½ cup lemon juice
¼ cup honey
2 pears
2 lemons, 1 pint strawberries-garnish
Ice

24 ounces lemon-lime soda
Yields 8 servings

1. Pour first five ingredients into a pitcher. Stir.
2. Add pears.
3. When ready pour 6 ounces sangria into fruit-garnished wine glasses half filled with ice.
4. Top with 3 ounces lemon-lime soda.

White Granny Smith Mint Sangria

Ingredients
1 750-milliliter bottle dry white wine
½ cup sour apple vodka
1 cup white cranberry juice
½ cup lemon juice
¼ cup sugar or simple syrup
1 cup peppermint sprigs
2 Granny Smith apples, 2 lemons
Ice

24 ounces soda water
Yields 8 servings

1. Pour first five ingredients into a pitcher. Stir.
2. Add fruit and mint to sangria.
3. When ready pour 6 ounces sangria into garnished wine glasses half filled with ice. Top each glass with 3 ounces soda water.

SANGRIAS

THEME WHITE SANGRIA

Learn how blondes have more fun when stirred up with festive creativity

The Tropical Luau Sangria can have so many flavorful substitutions and additions. Your favorite fruity flavored sprits like mango, pineapple, and mandarin can be used; shredded coconut and cherries are options; and sweeteners like coconut cream and sugar in place of the falernum would work. Falernum, by the way, is tropical syrup used in many exotic

drinks. It has a combination of flavors that includes vanilla, lime, almond, ginger, and cloves.

The goal of the Patriotic Sangria is to match the colors of the country of your choice; in this case, the country is America with blueberries, strawberries, and stars. France's colors are red, white, and blue, too, so the drink can be modified with

Tropical Luau Sangria

Ingredients
1 750-milliliter bottle dry white wine
½ cup coconut rum
½ cup white grape juice
½ cup pineapple juice
½ cup lemon juice
¼ cup falernum syrup
Assorted tropical fruits and flowers
Ice
24 ounces lemon-lime soda
Yields 8 servings

1. Pour the first six ingredients into a pitcher. Stir.
2. Add the fruit.
3. When ready pour 6 ounces sangria into garnished wine glasses half filled with ice.
4. Top with 3 ounces lemon-lime soda.

Patriotic Sangria

Ingredients
1 750-milliliter bottle dry American white wine
½ cup strawberry vodka
1 cup apple juice
½ cup lemon juice
¼ cup sugar or simple syrup
Strawberries, blueberries, and star fruit
Ice
24 ounces lemon-lime soda
Yields 8 servings

1. Pour first five ingredients into a pitcher. Stir.
2. Pour 6 ounces sangria into fruit-garnished wine glasses half filled with ice.
3. Top each glass with 3 ounces lemon-lime soda.

French white wine. Star fruit slices also can be colored with food coloring in the fridge overnight. Simply soak the fruit in the color of your choice mixed with water.

Pool Party Sangria incorporates blue Curacao so that it looks like pool water. Make citrus rings to look like swim rings and throw in some grapes for beach balls. If you don't have blue Curacao, substitute it with orange liqueur and blue food coloring. Also, you can easily change the name to "Under the Sea Sangria" or "Beach Party Sangria."

Before you make Down Under Sangria, check your local grocer for kiwi. Although many fruits like mango, papaya, and banana grow in Australia, the kiwi is its mascot fruit and simply cannot be left out of this theme sangria.

Have fun and come up with your own theme sangria! Ideas to spark your imagination include the Color Purple Sangria with violet syrup with plums and grapes, Billy Joel Sangria with a bottle of red and a bottle of white, or Kitchen Sink Sangria with whatever you have in your kitchen.

Pool Party Sangria

Ingredients
1 750-milliliter bottle dry white wine
½ cup blue Curacao
1 cup white grape juice
½ cup lemon juice
2 lemons, 2 oranges, pint of blueberries, and a cup of seedless grapes
Ice
24 ounces lemon-lime soda

Yields 8 servings

1. Pour first four ingredients into a pitcher. Stir.
2. Add fruit.
3. When ready pour 6 ounces sangria into garnished wine glasses half filled with ice.
4. Top with 3 ounces lemon-lime soda.

Down Under Sangria

Ingredients
1 750-milliliter bottle dry Australian white wine
½ cup mango vodka
1 cup white grape juice
½ cup lemon juice
¼ cup sugar or simple syrup
2 kiwi, 2 papayas, and 2 mangos
Ice
24 ounces soda water

Yields 8 servings

1. Pour first five ingredients into a pitcher. Stir.
2. Add fruit.
3. When ready pour 6 ounces sangria into garnished wine glasses half filled with ice.
4. Top each glass with 3 ounces soda water.

PINK SANGRIA

Tickle yourself and your friends pink by experimenting with rosy-hued wine

These days you'll find stores on the Internet that sell anything you want in the color pink. So why not have a pink sangria? Pink sangrias are perfect for a girls' night in, baby shower, bridal shower, bachelorette party, or for the person who loves pink or an event that is represented by the color pink. Wine choices include White Zinfandel, Rosé, and pink Champagne.

The Pretty in Pink Sangria is very versatile and can handle fun flavor changes with ease. You can experiment with cherry vodka with cherries, raspberry vodka or rum with raspberries, grape vodka with grapes, orange vodka with oranges, pear vodka with pears, and so forth.

Pretty in Pink Sangria

Ingredients
1 750-milliliter bottle White Zinfandel wine
½ cup limoncello
½ cup white cranberry juice
½ cup pink grapefruit juice
½ cup lemon juice
2 pink grapefruits, ½ cup lemon spirals, and 1 pint raspberries or strawberries
Ice

24 ounces Fresca grapefruit soda
Yields 8 servings

1. Pour first five ingredients into a pitcher. Stir.
2. Add pink grapefruit.
3. Pour 6 ounces sangria into fruit-garnished wine glasses half filled with ice; top each with 3 ounces Fresca soda.

Rose Parade Sangria

Ingredients
½ cup cherry vodka
¾ cup white grape juice
½ cup lemon juice
¼ cup rose simple syrup
1 cup white seedless grapes, 1 cup cherries, and 2 sliced lemons
Ice
2 750-milliliter bottles rosé brut Champagne

Yields 8 servings

1. Pour all ingredients except pink Champagne into a small pitcher. Stir gently.
2. When ready pour 2 ounces of the mixture into rose petal- and fruit-garnished wine glasses half filled with ice.
3. Slowly pour about 4 ounces pink Champagne on top.

The Rose Parade Sangria is a little different from all the other sangrias in this chapter because it combines the wine and carbonation by using Champagne (or sparkling wine). Feel free to combine it with any flavored spirit or liqueur of your choice. You won't be able to soak the fruit in this sangria because you can't pop the bottle until you're ready to serve.

Of course, any shape can be cut from watermelon meat, but the hearts in the Pink Heart Sangria give it a feeling that you made it with love. And love is always hip.

MAKE IT EASY

Know that cutting fruits into lots of different shapes takes extra prep time, but the visual presentation is priceless. If it's not the season for star fruit, for example, then you can slice up citrus wheels, then make angled cuts until you have a star shape. The rinds on the wheels can also be notched out with a knife for an interesting gear look.

Pink Heart Sangria

Ingredients
1 750-milliliter bottle rosé wine
½ cup watermelon schnapps
1 cup white grape juice
½ cup lemon juice
1 cup cantaloupe balls and 2 cups watermelon hearts
Ice
24 ounces soda water
Yields 8 servings

1. Pour the first four ingredients into a pitcher or large container. Stir.
2. Add the fruit, then let sit in the fridge for 3–12 hours.
3. When ready pour about 6 ounces of sangria into fruit-garnished wine glasses half filled with ice.
4. Top with 3 ounces soda water.

Watermelon Hearts

To make the watermelon hearts, start with a seedless watermelon. On a sturdy surface, slice half-inch watermelon rounds widthwise across the melon. If your knife is not long enough, simply cut the melon lengthwise first, then slice up half rounds. Cut rind off, then use a heart-shaped cookie cutter or paring knife to make the hearts.

175

TWISTED CLASSICS

Learn how to twist and shake up common cocktails into something new

Party drinks should be fun. There should always be something unique about a party drink, whether it's the color, garnish, flavor, name, and so forth. Your goal when presenting party drinks to guests is to see a look of excitement on their faces. When you see that look, then you know you've succeeded.

Party drinks are perfect for small gatherings of ten and fewer.

For more guests, I would suggest setting up a self-service table or bar with instructions and lots of prep work already taken care of. The best solution for larger crowds is to hire a bartender so you're not spending time cleaning the self serve table/bar or making drinks for your guests all night!

The best place to start with a party drink is a classic recipe

Twisted Tips

- You can replace the raspberry vodka with other flavored vodkas such as strawberry, grape, mango, mandarin, and orange.

- Don't be afraid of using a drop of food coloring in place of the grenadine in the Chocolate-tini. A rainbow of colors can be used!

- To keep apple slices fresh, soak them in lemon water or a product made for this task.

White Raspberry Cosmo

Ingredients

Ice
¾ ounce raspberry vodka
¾ ounce citrus vodka
¾ ounce Cointreau
½ ounce fresh lime juice
2 ounces white cranberry juice
Raspberry garnish

1. Chill a cocktail glass with ice.
2. Shake all the ingredients with ice.
3. Strain into the glass. Add garnish.

from a common cocktail. Then twist it. Here we started with a Cosmopolitan, Chocolate Martini, and an Appletini. The big twist on the Cosmo is using white cranberry juice in place of red cranberry juice. To bump up the flavor factor, we added raspberry vodka. "Pink chocolate" sounds intriguing, so by adding a little grenadine we achieve a whole new presentation. And who can resist the playfulness of a gummy worm through an apple slice?

MAKE IT EASY

If you don't have a friend to tend bar or a favorite bartender you can ask, then try contacting your local bartender school. Its students are always looking for real world practice to go with their new skills. Plus, they can be very economical, and you'll be able to request a specific gender or personality.

Pink Chocolate-tini

Ingredients

Shaved chocolate to rim glass
2 ounces vanilla vodka
1½ ounces white crème de cacao
¼ ounce grenadine

1. Rim a cocktail glass with shaved chocolate.
2. Shake all the ingredients with ice.
3. Strain into the glass.

Forbidden Appletini

Ingredients

Ice
2 ounces citrus vodka
2 ounces sour apple schnapps
Green apple slice and gummy worm garnish

1. Chill a cocktail glass with ice.
2. Shake all the ingredients with ice.
3. Strain into the glass. Add garnish.

FUN RIMMED PARTY DRINKS

Learn a myriad of ways you can rim a glass to grab immediate attention

Rimmed drinks scream fun, and fun is the main component needed for a great party drink. So far you've seen some great drinks in this book whose rims are crowned with assorted edibles. Now it's time to learn about other rimming possibilities.

The first thing to always consider is balancing the contents of the drink with the chosen rim ingredient. Both will be pro-

viding flavor and need to complement each other. For example, any cocktail with a sugar-based rim needs to have an element of sour for balance.

The very basic drink rims consist of coarse salt or sugar. Salt can be colored or mixed with a variety of flavors such as chili powder and other pepper powders, cracked espresso beans,

Ultraviolet

Ingredients

Purple sugar and edible purple glitter to rim glass
2 ounces Van Gogh açaí-blueberry vodka
¼ ounce Chambord raspberry liqueur
1 ounce lemon juice

1. Rim a cocktail glass with the purple sugar mixture.
2. Shake all the ingredients with ice.
3. Strain into the glass.

Pop Star

Ingredients

Strawberry Pop Rocks to rim glass
Ice
2 ounces green apple vodka
2 ounces strawberry pucker schnapps
1 ounce lemon juice
Star fruit slice garnish

1. Rim a cocktail glass with the strawberry Pop Rocks.
2. Shake all the ingredients with ice.
3. Strain into the glass. Add garnish.

citrus zest, and ginger, rosemary, mint, or sage. Sugar choices include using coarse, granulated, and superfine (baker's sugar). These can be colored or flavored with spices such as cinnamon, but sugar branches out much further because you can use cake sprinkles, hot chocolate powder, and any crushed candy imaginable such as red hots, lemon heads, lollipops, or any hard candy.

Other rimming choices include crushed nuts, shaved chocolate, frosted chopped cherries, shredded coconut, crushed cookies, or edible metallics.

MAKE IT EASY

Crush rimmed ingredients by putting them into a plastic bag and gently hitting with a heavy object. The ingredient chosen to stick your rimmed ingredients to the glass will require different sticking power. Salt and sugar rims can be rubbed with citrus or dipped into liquor or liqueurs. Cookies, coconut, and anything chunky requires something stickier like Karo syrup, chocolate syrup, or honey.

Insane Plantain

Ingredients

Lime zested salt to rim glass
1½ ounces reposado tequila
1 ounce banana liqueur
1 ounce lime juice

1. Rim a cocktail glass with lime zested salt.
2. Shake all the ingredients with ice.
3. Strain into the glass.

Ring of Fire (Birthday Drink)

Ingredients

Ice
2 ounces vanilla vodka
1 ounce Amaretto
1 ounce Amarula cream liqueur
3 ounces half-and-half
Assorted doughnuts and birthday candles for the special guest

1. Shake all the ingredients with ice.
2. Strain into the glass.
3. Set a doughnut on top of the drink.
4. Poke holes for the candles with a toothpick. Insert birthday candles.

FLOWER POWER PARTY DRINKS

Blooming ideas help you add an extra special taste to your cocktails

Flower power party drink ideas are plentiful! You can use flower-flavored spirits, liqueurs, syrups, waters, or garnishes to create flower-empowered drinks.

Market spirit and liqueur choices include elderflower liqueur, parfait amour, rose vodka, and crème de violette. You can also make your own flower-flavored spirits, syrups, and waters with fresh dried flowers or extracts of flowers.

Nontoxic flowers that can used in cocktails include dande-lion, rose, impatiens, violet, pansy, lilac, hibiscus, calendula, chamomile, marigold, cattail, gardenia, orchid, peony, chrysanthemum, carnation, gladiola, jasmine, snapdragon, tulip, and any flower from common culinary edibles like citrus and herbs. However, it's best to always gently wash pesticides off before using unless bought or grown organically.

Toxic flowers to never use include morning glory, lily of the valley, poinsettia, oleander, wisteria, sweet pea, azalea, daffo-

Wild about Hibiscus Flowers

Lee Etherington was the first to use the Australian wild hibiscus flowers in cocktails. It began at a dinner party in 1998 when he dropped a flower into a glass of Champagne. Before then the flower had been used as a popular Australian dessert garnish. Soon after Lee started the Wild Hibiscus Flower Company, which preserves his flowers in natural syrup for worldwide availability.

Tropical Hibiscus

Ingredients

Ice
1 ounce mango rum
1 ounce cranberry juice
1 ounce pineapple juice
½ ounce hibiscus syrup
3 ounces dry sparkling wine or brut Champagne
Sugarcane stick and a wild hibiscus flower turned inside out for garnish

1. Fill a tall glass with ice.
2. Shake the first four ingredients with ice.
3. Strain into the glass, then top with sparkling wine. Add garnish.

dil, hyacinth, mistletoe, periwinkle, rhododendron, foxglove, bird of paradise, narcissus, and nightshade.

The Tropical Hibiscus can be garnished with the wild hibiscus flower many ways. You can place it in the drink, float it on top of the drink, or skewer it. It would be perfect for a sunset beach wedding.

Perrier Jouet is the Champagne choice for Stop and Smell the Flowers because the bottle is handpainted with flowers, but you can substitute with another Champagne if desired.

ZOOM

The flowering tea buds in Blooming Jasmine Toddy are from China. They are handsewn into rosettes, open quickly when hot liquid is added to them, and come in many flavors. Make sure you choose a large, pretty, and thick glass with room for a hand to hold onto the toddy. Perfect for warming up a party in the dead of winter.

Stop and Smell the Flowers

Ingredients

Ice
½ ounce rose vodka
½ ounce elderflower liqueur
½ ounce violet liqueur
½ ounce lemon juice
4 ounces Perrier Jouet Champagne
Spray of rose water
Rose petal garnish

1. Fill a wine glass half with ice.
2. Add the first four ingredients.
3. Add Champagne, then spray the top of the drink with rose water.
4. Add garnish.

Blooming Jasmine Toddy

Ingredients

1½ ounces Bärenjäger honey liqueur or Wild Turkey Honey Liqueur
½ ounce lemon juice
Jasmine blooming tea flower
6 ounces hot water

1. Pour the honey liqueur and lemon juice into a thick glass.
2. Place a jasmine blooming tea flower in the bottom of the glass.
3. Pour in the hot water.

181

ICE & LIGHT DRINKS

Hot ice drinks and libations will light up your life

Nothing skyrockets a party mood faster than drinks that light up the night or the creative use of ice. Hopefully some of these ideas will help you spark ideas of your own.

Fortune Teller has an ice crystal ball that will be a great conversation starter for your guests. Ice balls can be purchased from Internet companies or made from molds found in novelty Japanese stores, or in a pinch you can freeze water-filled balloons. Keep the balloon shape as round as possible.

Ice cones frozen around straws have been around in tiki bars since the 1950s. Make your own by packing a paper snow cone cup with crushed ice, adding water (or juice), then sticking a pencil or chopstick in the middle to make a hole for the straw.

Tap water freezes cloudy because of chemicals and air bubbles. To make your ice creations as clear as possible, use filtered water. For crystal-clear ice, boil filtered water, then al-

Fortune Teller

Tiki Traffic Cone

Ingredients

Ice and Ice ball
2 ounces Hpnotiq
1 ounce VooDoo spiced rum

1. Chill a cocktail glass with ice.
2. Place an ice ball into a cocktail glass.
3. Shake all the ingredients with ice.
4. Strain in the glass. Read your fortune.

Ingredients

Orange juice straw cone
Ice
1½ ounces dark rum
½ ounce orgeat syrup (or Amaretto)
1 ounce red passion fruit syrup
1 ounce pineapple juice
1 ounce lime juice

1. Place the straw cone in a highball glass wide enough to fit the cone.
2. Shake all the ingredients with ice.
3. Strain into the glass.

low it to cool. Boil it again, and then it's ready to use.

Other fun ice you can try is dry ice. Put a large chunk into the bottom of a thick glass, then add ice on top of the chunk. Never store dry ice in an airtight container or touch it with your bare hands, especially if they are wet. Follow these simple precautions, and all will be fine. You can also freeze edibles in ice cube trays for extra fun. Try berries, coffee beans, herbs, fruits, and so forth.

Starry Starry Night will appeal to artists everywhere. It was inspired by Van Gogh's most popular painting, which was painted while he was in an asylum in 1889. To make "black" black cherry vodka, simply add 3 drops of black food coloring to a bottle of Van Gogh's black cherry vodka.

Starry Starry Night

Ingredients

Blue ice cube lights
Ice
½ ounce blue Curacao
½ ounce lemon juice
4 ounces lemon-lime soda
1½ ounces Van Gogh black black cherry vodka
Lemon wheel

1. Place a blue light cube into the bottom of a tall glass, then fill with ice.
2. Pour in the blue Curacao, lemon juice, and soda water.
3. Slowly layer the black black cherry vodka on top.
4. Add another blue light cube and a wheel of lemon.

Mexican Glow Worm

Ingredients

Ice
1½ ounces blanco tequila
1 ounce melon liqueur
1 ounce lime juice
½ ounce agave syrup
4 ounces soda water
Glow necklace

1. Slowly spiral a glow necklace into a bottomed bowled glass like a snifter as you add ice.
2. Shake the next four ingredients with ice.
3. Strain into the glass, then top with soda water.

FUN GARNISH PARTY DRINKS

Keep the party lighthearted by taking a little time to make some fun garnishes

Garnishes are the crowning touch to a drink, and guests always love to see something out of the ordinary sitting on top of or in their cocktail.

Everyone loves fortune cookies because they add a sense of whimsical magic. Why not dip some in chocolate? You could even add sprinkles and other decorations to them. Sloe Boat

to China is the perfect tall, cool drink to set a dipped fortune cookie on its rim.

The Black Leather String Bikini is a simple drink that smells like suntan lotion. If you prefer a Red Leather String Bikini, simply use red shoestring licorice in place of the black.

You'll need to make a cardboard template to make the gar-

Sloe Boat to China

Ingredients

Ice
1 ounce sloe gin
1 ounce white crème de cacao
4 ounces soda water
Chocolate-dipped fortune cookie

1. Fill a tall glass with ice.
2. Shake the next two ingredients with ice.
3. Strain into the glass, then top with soda water. Add garnish.

Black Leather String Bikini

Ingredients

Ice
2 ounces coconut rum
5 ounces white cranberry juice
Black shoestring licorice

1. Slowly spiral black shoestring licorice into a tall glass as you add ice.
2. Shake ingredients with ice.
3. Strain into the glass.

nish for the Yin Yang-tini. A sheet of cardstock or poster cardboard will work fine. Simply turn your chosen glass upside down on the cardboard and trace around the edge. Now draw the yin-yang design and cut it out. The chocolate discs/wafers can be found at cake supply stores or mall candy stores. You can make your own by melting chocolate, spreading it out on wax paper, and allowing it to cool. When ready, find something around the kitchen like a condiment cap to use as a cutter to make round chocolate wafers.

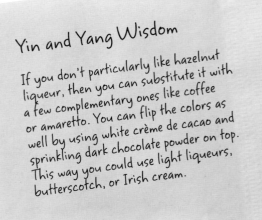

MAKE IT EASY

Other fun garnish ideas include stencils that fit the party's occasion, melon balls, chocolate-covered strawberries, a maple leaf for a drink that has maple syrup, half an orange shell in a drink, using shaped hole punches on citrus rinds, and using cookie cutters to make shapes with fruit. You'll also find lots of ideas at candy stores.

Yin Yang-tini

Ingredients

Ice
2 ounces vanilla vodka
2 ounces dark crème de cacao
1 ounce hazelnut liqueur
1 ounce half-and-half
Shredded white chocolate
and chocolate discs

1. Cut half of a yin-yang template from cardboard based on the size of your chosen glass.
2. Blend all the ingredients with half a cup of ice.
3. Pour into the glass.
4. Place the cardboard template over half of the top of the glass and sprinkle shredded white chocolate. Place the chocolate discs on top of the drink.

Yin and Yang Wisdom

If you don't particularly like hazelnut liqueur, then you can substitute it with a few complementary ones like coffee or amaretto. You can flip the colors as well by using white crème de cacao and sprinkling dark chocolate powder on top. This way you could use light liqueurs, butterscotch, or Irish cream.

SPECIAL-TOUCH PARTY DRINKS
Make some party drinks that require your extra personal touch

Sometimes party drinks require an extra touch. We've all seen the drink markers, rings, and tags to keep everyone's drinks organized, so why not try some other ideas? One idea is to stick some of those translucent, rubbery window clings onto glasses. They come in a variety of designs and can be found in arts and crafts stores. They can even be cut down to size.

The cocktail Kiss My Glass is a clever idea to try. Simply slather on some lipstick and kiss the glass where your lips can fit.

Make sure to leave enough unkissed surface that the drink can be held without lipstick getting all over someone's hand. This drink would be great for Valentine's Day, an anniversary, a romantic evening, or just to flirt with the cutie across the room.

The Lucky Lady Bug looks just like a lady bug. It can also possibly be called the "watermelon" because it tastes like watermelon, and the chocolate dots look like watermelon

Kiss My Glass

Ingredients

Dark pink, red, or white lipstick kisses on outside of glass
Ice
2 ounces X-Rated vodka
2 ounces X-Rated fusion liqueur

1. Kiss the outside of a glass with lipstick.
2. Fill half with ice.
3. Shake the ingredients with ice.
4. Strain into the glass.

Lucky Lady Bug

Ingredients

Dark chocolate
Ice
2 ounces Southern Comfort
1 ounce crème de noyeaux
2 ounces orange juice

1. Melt chocolate in a microwave.
2. Dip middle finger in chocolate and make dots inside a cocktail glass. Double coat if necessary.
3. Put glass in freezer to set.
4. Shake ingredients with ice and strain into the glass.

seeds. You can experiment with lots of polka-dotted things! How about making a yellow drink and calling it the "Itsy Bitsy Teenie Weenie Polka Dotted Bikini"? You could use white chocolate, too. And white chocolate can be made into any color, so that leaves everything up to your imagination.

MAKE IT EASY

You'll need to make the *Message Martini* clear or white to be able to read the message. You can also experiment with other colored thick syrups on the market. The little tubes of cake frosting work well, too. Just make sure that you strain the drink into the glass very slowly so as not to disturb your message.

Message Martini

Ingredients

Chocolate syrup
Ice
2 ounces chocolate vodka
2 ounces white chocolate liqueur
1 ounce half-and-half

1. Write message inside a cocktail glass with chilled chocolate syrup.
2. Shake the ingredients with ice.
3. Slowly strain into the glass.

Chocolate Design Tips

- Transfer chocolate syrup to condiment bottles for better control.

- Chilled chocolate syrup writes better and lasts longer.

- For more control, paint with chocolate using a small paintbrush.

- Place glasses in freezer to set.

- Use letters or numbers to write message that fits the occasion. Remember that you'll have to write words backward.

HISTORICAL PUNCH

Stir up some vintage bowls of century-old libations from our ancestors

Punch has been recorded in history since the 1500s. Many people believe that the word *punch* came from the Hindu word *panch*. We know that the drink made its way to the New World in the 1600s because it was documented in menus, letters, and even George Washington's diary.

Fish House Punch got its start among many of the founding

fathers and their friends in Philadelphia in the 1700s. These influential men started their own boys' club (okay, gentlemen's club) and called it "State in Schuylkill Fishing Corporation." They built themselves a clubhouse near the Schuylkill river, created a special punch, and established the motto "Fish, drink, and eat!" The club is still around today. It has moved a

Fish House Punch

Ingredients
4 cups fresh squeezed lime juice
2 cups fresh squeezed lemon juice
1 cup water
5 cups brown sugar
1 750-milliliter chilled bottle dark Jamaica rum
1 750-milliliter chilled bottle light rum
1 750-milliliter chilled bottle peach brandy
Block of ice
Yields 20–25 servings

1. Mix the juices, brown sugar, and water together until all the sugar has dissolved.
2. Add the alcohol, then stir.
3. Serve in a bowl with a block of ice.

Wassail

Ingredients
½ gallon unfiltered apple cider or juice
2 cups cranberry juice
½ cup brown sugar
12 whole cloves
12 allspice berries
6 cinnamon sticks
3 large apples, chopped
1 large orange, chopped
1 750-milliliter bottle sherry
2 bottles brown ale
Yields 20–25 servings

1. Put the first 9 ingredients into a large pot. Set stove on low.
2. Cook on low to simmer 1 hour.
3. Add sherry and brown ale. Stir gently.
4. Transfer to a crock pot set on low.

few times and has had many names over the years, including "Castle," "Colony in Schuylkill," and "Fish House." For the record, it is the oldest gentlemen's club in continuous existence in the world.

Wassail is a word from the Middle Ages that basically translates to the popular toast "to your health!" Wassail was also a common community tradition in which people walked door to door with a big wooden bowl while singing (caroling), then yelling out "Wassail!" as neighbors filled their bowl with ingredients to make punch.

PUNCHES

MAKE IT EASY

Keep in mind that all punch recipes can be modified to fit your guest list. Simply guesstimate how many drinks your guests may drink, then adjust the recipe by doubling or halving the ingredients in the recipe. Punch servings are normally around 6 ounces.

Whiskey Milk Punch

Pegleg Sullivan

It is believed that on October 8, 1871, Daniel "Pegleg" Sullivan started the Chicago fire, which killed hundreds of people, burned 4 square miles, and burned for three days. He was reported to have been stealing milk from a cow to make Whiskey Milk Punch when the cow kicked a lantern into the hay.

Ingredients
2 750-milliliter chilled bottles blended American whiskey
¾ gallon whole milk
2 cups sugar
¼ cup nutmeg
Extra nutmeg for garnish
Yields 20 servings

1. Mix everything together in a large pitcher.
2. Place in fridge until ready to serve.
3. Pour cold into glass cups.
4. Sprinkle a little nutmeg on top.

ICE CREAM PUNCH
Have fun making some creamy subzero punches for your next party

Everything on the serving table for the root beer float punch must be cold. First, clear out a space in the freezer to line up your glasses or mugs. Pour the vodka and schnapps into a pitcher, then place it and the root beer in the fridge. Fifteen minutes before your guests arrive you will need three large containers or bowls of ice on the punch table that will hold the glasses or mugs, ice cream, and root beer. Set the pitcher on the table and have plenty of straws, long-handled spoons (spoon straws would be a nice touch), and napkins on the table

Another presentation idea for the vodka and schnapps would be to funnel the mixture back into the bottles, then freeze a block of ice around the bottles. All you need is an empty rinsed half-gallon juice or milk carton. Just cut the top off, then set the bottle inside, fill with water, and freeze (the mixture won't freeze solid). When ready, simply tear off the

Root Beer Float Punch

Ingredients
1 750-milliliter bottle vanilla vodka
1 750-milliliter bottle root beer schnapps
1 quart vanilla ice cream
4 liters cold root beer
Yields 20–25 servings

1. Pour the vodka and schnapps into a pitcher and chill in the fridge.
2. When ready pour 2 ounces of the cold pitcher mixture into frozen glasses or mugs.
3. Add 1 scoop of ice cream in each glass or mug.
4. Top with chilled root beer.

Tropical Rainbow Punch

Ingredients
1 750-milliliter chilled bottle coconut rum
½ gallon chilled pineapple juice
1 pint multicolored sherbet
2 liters chilled ginger ale
Pineapple flags garnish
Yields 20–25 servings

1. Pour the first two ingredients into a pitcher and chill in the fridge.
2. When ready pour chilled mixture into a punch bowl.
3. Set the sherbet in the middle of the punch, then pour in the chilled ginger ale. Add garnish.

paper, and you'll have a block of ice around a bottle. Pop a pourer on top, and you're ready to set it on a deep dish on the table. Your guests will love the extra-effort presentation.

•••••••••• GREEN ● LIGHT ••••••••••

Feel free to add rainbow or tropical theme elements to the Tropical Rainbow Punch table. Maybe set everything on top of a grass skirt or elephant ear. Another idea is to place rainbow-colored ice cream cones in the bottom of punch glasses for a festive presentation around the bowl. You can find the assorted colored cones at your grocer.

Fried Coffee Punch

Ingredients

1 750-milliliter bottle coffee liqueur
1 750-milliliter bottle Irish cream
½ gallon cold coffee
½ quart vanilla and ½ quart chocolate ice cream pressed together and frozen
2 ounces 151 rum
½ ounce cinnamon garnish

Yields 20–25 servings

1. Pour first three ingredients into a large container.
2. When ready pour; chill mixture into a glass punch bowl.
3. Set ice cream in the middle of the punch.
4. Pour 151 rum on top of ice cream, light, then sprinkle on cinnamon.

Fried Coffee Punch Tips

• Dim the lights after igniting the ice cream because the cinnamon sprinkle will create a minifireworks show for your guests.

• Always take full precautions when working with fire. Make sure there is nothing flammable around the punch. Do not serve until fire has died.

• Rubber gloves help when working with the ice cream.

GLOBAL PUNCH

Try using ingredients represented by countries from around the planet

Punch doesn't have to be served in a big bowl. Pitchers can work as well. You can always have backup pitchers in the fridge ready to pull out as one empties. For parties on the go or outdoors, large water coolers with spigots work very well. Of course, these types of containers can be a little unattractive for a theme party, so feel free to cover and embellish

them. Indoors you can also use clear three-gallon water containers with spigots or large glass jars with spigots.

Keeping punch cold is a main concern. Back in the day, our founding fathers chipped blocks from frozen lakes to throw into the bowl. Today, thanks to modern conveniences, there are many creative ways to keep the punch cold. One of the

American Punch

Ingredients
2 cups Southern Comfort
2 cups Jack Daniel's
2 cups orange juice
2 cups pineapple juice
1 cup lemon juice
½ cup grenadine
Ice
Cherries garnish
Yields 10 servings

1. Pour all the ingredients into a pitcher and stir.
2. Chill punch in the fridge until ready.
3. When ready fill tall glasses with ice.
4. Pour in the punch. Add garnish.

German Punch

Ingredients
2 cups Jägermeister
2 cups peach schnapps
2 cups cranberry juice
2 cups pineapple juice
1 cup lemon juice
Ice
Peach garnish
Yields 10 servings

1. Pour all the ingredients into a pitcher and stir.
2. Chill punch in the fridge until ready.
3. When ready fill tall glasses with ice.
4. Pour in the punch. Add garnish.

most popular is to freeze water in a ring mold to float in the bowl. But you don't have to freeze only water. Why not freeze some of the mixer being used in the punch? You can also throw in some of the garnishes. More ideas include freezing garnishes in ice cube trays, freezing mixers in ice cube trays, using freezable plastic ice cubes, and using a bowl made of ice (see Ice Bowl Punch).

MAKE IT EASY

Every large city has several Asian supermarkets. Several brands of canned lychees in syrup can be found in Asian market fruit aisles, and fresh lychees can be found in the produce aisle or sometimes at the checkout stand. The fresh lychees will be red and joined together on a vine like grapes.

French Punch

Ingredients
1 750-milliliter bottle strawberry vodka
1 750-milliliter bottle Chambord
1 cup Grand Marnier
1 cup cranberry juice
1 cup lemon juice
1 bottle French Champagne
Ice
Strawberry garnish

Yields 20 servings

1. Pour all the ingredients except the Champagne into a pitcher and stir.
2. Chill in the fridge until ready.
3. When ready pour into wine glasses filled three-fourths full of ice.
4. Top with chilled Champagne. Add garnish.

Asian Punch

Ingredients
1 750-milliliter bottle sake
1 750-milliliter bottle lychee liqueur
1 750-milliliter bottle Hangar One Citron Buddha's Hand vodka
1 gallon white cranberry juice
Ice
1 2-liter bottle chilled ginger ale

Lychee or fortune cookie garnish
Yields 40–50 servings

1. Pour first four ingredients into a large container and stir.
2. Chill in the fridge until ready.
3. Pour into wine glasses filled three-fourths full of ice.
4. Top with chilled ginger ale. Add garnish.

ICE BOWL PUNCH
Chill out and impress your guests with your ice-sculpting skills

One of the main challenges with punch served in bowls is keeping the punch cold. As mentioned before, you can make ice molds using just about anything with water or mixer or even throw in a block of ice like our founding fathers did. But why not make the bowl out of ice? How cool is that? You can also freeze all kinds of items in the bowl to match a theme.

The only real issue with an ice bowl is what to set it on to absorb or drain the water when it is on the punch table. The best solution I've found is diapers. The chemical inside diapers is sodium polyacrylate, and it's very absorbent. Simply open a few diapers flat over and around a plate, then lay a fun piece of material over the diapers and set the ice bowl on the plate. Decorate around the bowl.

Tap water was used for the Bowl of Cherries Punch and Patriotic Punch. To achieve crystal-clear ice seen in the Garden Party Punch, you will have to prepare the water. All you do is

Ice Bowl Mold

- You need a large plastic bowl and a smaller plastic bowl to nest inside.

- Fill the large bowl half with water. More can be added later.

- Weight the smaller bowl inside the larger with a rock and wet kitchen towels.

- Tape to secure and freeze. When needed, thaw for 15 minutes, and the bowls will pop off.

Bowl of Cherries Punch

Ingredients

1 750-milliliter bottle cherry vodka
½ gallon pink lemonade
1 2-liter bottle Fresca
Yields 20–25 servings

1. Mix the vodka and lemonade in a pitcher. Chill in the fridge.
2. When ready pour the vodka and lemonade into the ice bowl three-quarters of the way up.
3. Top with cold Fresca.
4. Replenish as needed.

boil a large pot of water, then allow it to cool. Bring it to a boil again, and then it's ready.

The ice in this drink is crystal-clear.

Garden Party Punch

Ingredients

1 750-milliliter bottle St-Germain elderflower liqueur
1 750-milliliter bottle pear vodka
4 bottles brut Champagne
Yields 20–25 servings

1. Mix the liqueur and vodka together in a pitcher. Chill in the fridge.
2. When ready split the pitcher mixture into four equal parts.
3. Pour one of the parts into the ice bowl and top off with a chilled bottle of Champagne.
4. Replenish as needed using this ratio.

Patriotic Punch

Ingredients

1 750-milliliter bottle strawberry vodka
2 cups blue Curacao
½ gallon lemonade
1 2-liter bottle lemon-lime soda
Yields 20–25 servings

1. Mix the vodka, blue Curacao, and lemonade in a pitcher. Chill in the fridge.
2. When ready pour the mixture in the ice bowl three-quarters of the way up.
3. Top with cold lemon-lime soda.
4. Replenish as needed.

WARM PUNCH

Heat up your party by mixing batches of punch on those cold, wintry days

When it's cold outside, nothing warms friends' hearts more than whipping up a batch of warm punch.

This Hot Buttered Rum recipe is made without adding the dark rum to the mix on purpose. Some guests may not want the alcohol for various reasons, and others may want to add as little or as much as they please. You'll also notice that there are three ways to use the mix. If you decide to keep it in a container in the fridge, then know that it should stay good for one month. For the Spicy Fruit Punch, you can also add fruits such as chopped apples, oranges, and pineapples. And the cranapple juice can be replaced with equal parts of cranberry juice and apple juice.

Hot Buttered Rum Mix Ideas

The mix can be added to a gallon of hot water on the stove, then poured into a crock pot. It can also be placed into ice cube trays, then frozen. After it is frozen, simply pop out and store in a freezer bag until ready to use. When ready, drop one cube into a cup, add the amount of rum you'd like, then fill with hot water.

Hot Buttered Rum

Ingredients

3 cups brown sugar
1 cup unsalted butter, softened
1 ounce honey
1 tablespoon ground cinnamon
1 tablespoon ground cloves
1 tablespoon ground nutmeg
1 quart vanilla ice cream, softened

1 750-milliliter bottle dark rum
Yields 20–25 servings

1. Pour all the ingredients except the dark rum into a large bowl. Mix together. Keep mixture in the fridge until ready.
2. Scoop 2 tablespoons of mix into a coffee mug.
3. Add 1 ounce dark rum, then fill with hot water. Stir.

Gingerbread cookies can be served alongside the Gingerbread House Punch if desired. You can also use a variety of candy sticks as stir stick garnishes. To save some calories, you can replace the eggnog with light eggnog. The chai tea in 32-ounce cartons can be found at your local grocer in the health section.

Always keep in mind that warm punches can be poured into crock pots set on low. Simply supply your guests with a ladle, cups, and mugs, garnishes, if any, and napkins.

MAKE IT EASY

Why not invite friends over for a gingerbread gathering? Serve the Gingerbread House Punch while making gingerbread man cookies. Or you can make gingerbread houses, then hold a contest for best gingerbread house. Simply supply assorted candy in bowls, frosting, tools, tubed frosting, and gingerbread squares. You can also build a house using graham crackers.

Spicy Fruit Punch

Gingerbread House Punch

Ingredients

1 cup brown sugar
20 whole cloves
4 sticks cinnamon
1 46-ounce bottle cranapple juice
2 cups pineapple juice
2 cups water
1 750-milliliter bottle Tuaca
2 cups Grand Marnier

Star anise garnish
Yields 20–25 servings

1. Pour all the ingredients except the Tuaca and Grand Marnier into a large pot.
2. Heat on low for 1 hour, then strain cloves and sticks.
3. Stir in the Tuaca and Grand Marnier.
4. Ladle into cups. Add garnish.

Ingredients

2 32-ounce cartons liquid chai tea
3 cups eggnog
1 750-milliliter bottle ginger liqueur
Cinnamon sticks or candy cane garnish

1. Pour all the ingredients except the ginger liqueur into a large pot.
2. Heat on low until warm.
3. Stir in the ginger liqueur.
4. Ladle into cups. Add garnish.

THEME FOUNTAIN PUNCH
Create a centerpiece of flowing liquid goodness for all to enjoy

What better way to get the party started than to create a towering libation waterfall? Not only is it pleasing to the eyes, but also its trickling sound is soothing to the ears.

These fountain punch examples are themed to help give you some ideas for your party. Other occasions when a fountain would be appropriate are a graduation of any kind, bachelorette or retirement party, bridal shower, reunion, anniversary, homecoming, or any event that attracts a room of

people. Try to set the fountain on a table away from the wall so that it can be approached from all sides. This setting commands attention and encourages conversation.

You should know a few things about fountains. First, you need to decide whether to buy or rent a fountain. For about $50, party stores rent small to extra-large, grandiose fountains that will keep up to five gallons of punch cold because they contain a chiller. Until recently this was the only way to ex-.

Wedding Punch

Ingredients

Yields 50–60 servings

3 750-milliliter bottles Amaretto
1 750-milliliter bottle vanilla rum or vodka
3 gallons whole milk
½ gallon half-and-half
¼ cup ground nutmeg
Frozen milk cubes and clear light cubes

Option 1. Mix all ingredients together, then funnel into gallon jugs. Refrigerate.
Option 2. When ready fill bowl with punch. Add more as needed.

Birthday Punch

Ingredients

2 750-milliliter bottles dark rum
2 750-milliliter bottles spiced rum
1 gallon pineapple juice
1 gallon pulp-free orange juice
1 gallon lemonade
2 cups grenadine

Frozen ice balloons
Yields 40–50 servings

Option 1. Mix all ingredients together, then funnel into gallon jugs. Refrigerate.
Option 2. Fill fountain bowl with cold white cranberry juice. Either add cold vodka into the bowl or set beside the bowl.

perience a fountain, and you normally saw one only at weddings. Today several small to medium, clear acrylic fountains are available to the public for around $50. They work very well but don't contain a chiller. The wedding punch (that tastes like wedding cake) is kept cold with frozen milk cubes. The birthday punch is kept chilly with frozen balloons. Hint: Let the balloons thaw a little so that the rubber thickens before placing them in the fountain. For the baby shower punch, the rubber duckies were filled with water and frozen. Always think about creative ways to keep punch chilled without too much dilution and always keep backup punch in the fridge for refilling. For mixed drinking crowds you can add the cold mixer to the bowl and set the alcohol next to the bowl allowing guests to choose to add or not add alcohol.

Baby Shower Punch

Ingredients

2 750-milliliter bottles raspberry vodka
2 750-milliliter bottles citrus vodka
3 gallons white cranberry juice
3–6 drops blue food coloring
Rubber duckies
Yields 40–50 servings

Option 1. Mix all ingredients together, then funnel into gallon jugs. Refrigerate.
Option 2. Fill fountain bowl with cold white cranberry juice. Either add cold vodka into the bowl or set beside the bowl.

Fountain Punch Tips

- Never pour into the fountain anything with pulp, seeds, gelatin, or ice cream or anything small and chunky. Doing so will ruin the motor.

- Never let the fountain run dry because doing so will burn up the motor.

- Know that fountains shown here need 2–3 gallons of liquid to start.

MODERN VODKA COCKTAILS
Discover possibilities using ingredients made from herbs and flowers

The first golden age of cocktails occurred during the first twenty years of the twentieth century. Barmen took the artform of crafting vintage cocktails and new creations very seriously. But all this ended in 1920 because of Prohibition. Eighty years later, around the millennium, the cocktail entered its second golden age. Bartenders and enthusiasts worldwide

united to help preserve the craft of the cocktail. A museum was even established to celebrate this American icon. You can visit online at museumoftheamericancocktail.org.

Cocktails of today began simply from the desire to use the freshest ingredients possible. Soon after there was a marriage of the kitchen and the bar, resulting in new buzzwords like

Oz

Ingredients

Ice
1½ ounces rose petal and blue poppy seed-infused premium orange vodka
1 ounce Green Chartreuse
1 ounce fresh Meyer lemon juice
1 mist of rose water

1. Chill a 4–6-ounce cocktail glass with ice.
2. Shake all ingredients with ice except the rose water.
3. Strain into a cocktail glass.
4. Spray a mist of rose water across the top of the drink.

Dusk

Ingredients

Ice
½ ounce pear vodka
1 ounce St-Germain elderflower liqueur
1 ounce crème de violette
1 ounce fresh Meyer lemon juice

1. Chill a 4–6-ounce cocktail glass with ice.
2. Stir all ingredients with ice.
3. Strain into a cocktail glass.

bar chef and mixologist. This marriage soon led to researching and mastering the vintage cocktails from the 1800s and early 1900s.

Imaginative avant-garde mixologists today experiment with pink peppercorns, lemongrass, truffles, squid ink, and bacon. They also incorporate historic ingredients such as bitters, falernum, absinthe, and a variety of vermouths. Popular techniques include pureeing, muddling, misting, foaming, infusing, double straining, and suspending. Other ingredients you may find in a modern cocktail include herbs such as sage, rosemary, and cilantro, flowers such as hibiscus, rose, elderflower, and lavender, and fruits such as lychee, jackfruit, and calamamci.

The Oz gets its name from the poppy seeds and flower petals used to infuse the orange vodka as well as the Green Chartreuse, whose color is reminiscent of the Emerald City.

When the sun is 6 degrees below the horizon, it produces dreamy colors across the evening sky. This time of day is called "dusk." The Dusk cocktail looks like one of those colors. The crème de violette was extinct for many years but has now been resurrected thanks to modern bartender efforts.

Tainted Virtue

Ingredients

Ice
1½ ounces Madagascar vanilla bean-infused vodka
½ ounce Drambuie
½ ounce raw simple syrup
1 ounce cold espresso
2 ounces fresh cream garnish

1. Chill a 4–6-ounce cocktail glass with ice.
2. Shake all ingredients with ice.
3. Strain into the cocktail glass.

Green Chartreuse

Green Chartreuse is a liqueur that is made from 130 herbs. It has been made by monks since 1605 and was finally perfected in 1764. Fans of Chartreuse include Bon Jovi, the Smithereens, and the late Queen Elizabeth Bowes-Lyon. It was also mentioned in the novel *The Great Gatsby* (1925) and seen in the film *Grindhouse* (2007).

201

MODERN GIN COCKTAILS
Shake and strain the old and the new to create some delectable libations

Gin is one of the spirits that modern mixologists love to experiment with because it embodies many herbs and botanicals and it has been written up in cocktail recipe books since 1862.

Modern bartenders love marrying fresh ideas with historic ingredients, and the Gypsy Bloodless Mary is a great example.

The original Bloody Mary was made with gin, and this modern cocktail is a little twist on this tomato-based libation . . . without the tomato. Noilly Prat French dry vermouth has been handcrafted in the south of France in the small village of Marseillan on the Mediterranean coast since 1813. Celery bitters can be found in historic cocktail books but has not

Gypsy Bloodless Mary

Ingredients

Ice
2 ounces cucumber-infused gin
½ ounce Noilly Prat dry
2 dashes The Bitter Truth Celery Bitters
Celery salt rim and cucumber or celery garnish

1. Chill a 4–6-ounce cocktail glass with ice, then rim with celery salt.
2. Stir all ingredients with ice.
3. Strain into the cocktail glass. Add garnish.

Pineapple Butterscotch Collins

Ingredients

Ice
1 ounce Hawaiian pineapple-infused gin
1 ounce butterscotch schnapps
1 ounce Hawaiian pineapple puree
1 ounce fresh Meyer lemon juice

4 ounces fresh charged soda water.
Pineapple garnish

1. Shake the first four ingredients with ice.
2. Strain into a tall glass or Collins glass of ice.
3. Fill with fresh charged soda water. Add garnish.

been available (commercially at least) since the mid-1900s. The Bitter Truth Celery Bitters is a recent introduction (2006), invented by Stephan Berg and Alexander Hauck in Munich. An online search will yield sites to obtain it in the U.S.. To make the lengthwise cucumber slice garnish, you will definitely need a slicer.

To make fresh charged soda water for the Pineapple Butterscotch Collins, you'll need to invest in a soda siphon. The first soda siphon was patented in 1829 and used for many cocktails until the 1940s. This is why you see it in films from the 1930s–1940s. The commercial production of seltzer/soda water was the cause of the decline of the soda siphon, but modern bartenders love resurrecting vintage barware, so the modern soda siphon can be found in all cocktail bars dedicated to the craft. You simply fill it with filtered water and attach the charger, and it's ready to go.

Loose honeysuckle tea can be found at local teashops or online. To avoid bitterness, don't infuse the gin for the Suckle with the tea more than four hours.

Suckle

Ingredients

Ice
2 ounces loose honeysuckle tea-infused gin
1 ounce Rhum Clément Créole Shrubb
1 ounce fresh lemon juice
2 dashes Angostura bitters

1. Chill a cocktail glass with ice.
2. Shake all the ingredients with ice.
3. Strain into the chilled cocktail glass.

Rhum Clément Creole Shrubb

Rhum Clément Créole Shrubb is an orange Curaçao liqueur that is mixed with Caribbean spices. It became available in America in 2007. It has been made on the east coast of Martinique since the late 1800s and was invented by the French physician Homère Clément, who brought his distilling knowledge with him when he moved to Martinique.

MODERN RUM COCKTAILS

Create extraordinary rum cocktails using out-of-the-ordinary ingredients

The cocktail name, Kong, is a play on the banana rum and the strong flavor of the coffee. You can use any type of espresso beans you desire, but experts say that Arabica beans have a balanced compromise of flavor. The cacao nips are the beans that chocolate is made from. If you don't have the time to wait for all these beans to infuse your banana rum, then just

use add ½ ounce chocolate liqueur in the recipe to make up for the chocolate taste to get an idea of what it will taste like. The pure vanilla whipped cream is achieved by adding a cap of pure vanilla as you are whipping the cream. Look for Mexican chocolate in local Spanish or Caribbean stores. This chocolate is unlike any chocolate you've ever tasted. It's

Strong Kong

Ingredients

1 ounce Arabica espresso bean and roasted cacao nip-infused banana rum
1 ounce coffee liqueur
5 ounces fresh hot coffee
1 teaspoon brown sugar
Pure vanilla extract, whipped cream, and Mexican chocolate chunk garnish

1. Pour all the ingredients into a coffee glass.
2. Stir. Add garnish.

Rhuby Slipper

Ingredients

Ice
1½ ounce rhubarb and strawberry-infused gold rum
1 ounce fresh Persian lime juice
1 ounce falernum
4 ounces dry white wine
2 ounces fresh charged filtered water

Fanned strawberry garnish

1. Fill a medium wine glass half with ice.
2. Add all the ingredients except for the fresh charged water. Stir.
3. Top with fresh charged water. Add garnish.

mixed with spices and coarse-grained sugar.

When infusing the gold rum with rhubarb and strawberries to make the Rhuby Slipper, make sure you do not put the rhubarb leaves into the infusion because they are toxic. The stalk is the only part that is nontoxic. Gardeners know to grow rhubarb on the outskirts of their garden for this reason. Falernum is the sweetening agent in this cocktail. It can be found in gourmet shops or online. You can also make the Rhuby Slipper by substituting the infused vodka with 1 ounce strawberry vodka and 1 ounce rhubarb liqueur, then

use only ½ ounce of the falernum.

When infusing the mango rum for the Heatwave, crack the peppercorns a little by placing them in a plastic bag and giving them a couple of good hits with something heavy. A variety of peppercorn types can be found in gourmet stores. Rainbow peppercorn can be found as a mixture of white, black, pink, and green peppercorns.

Heatwave

Heatwave Garnish

Ingredients

Fresh-ground cinammon and organic sugar to rim glass
Ice
2 ounces rainbow peppercorn-infused mango rum
1 ounce tropical fruit puree
1 ounce fresh Meyer lemon juice
2 dashes Angostura bitters

Mini-mango checkerboard cut arched garnish

1. Rim a chilled cocktail glass with the cinnamon sugar.
2. Shake all the ingredients with ice.
3. Strain into the glass. Add mini-mango garnish.

Wild Hibiscus Mojito

Ingredients

3 wild hibiscus flowers in syrup and 3 peppermint sprigs
1 ounce peppermint leaf and Persian lime zest-infused light rum
1 ounce fresh Persian lime juice
1 ounce wild hibiscus syrup
Ice
4 ounces fresh charged filtered

water
1 ounce gold rum
Peppermint stem, inside-out wild hibiscus flower garnish

1. Muddle flowers and peppermint in a tall glass.
2. Add infused rum, lime juice, and syrup. Fill with ice and fresh charged filtered water.
3. Float gold rum. Add garnish.

MODERN TEQUILA COCKTAILS

Go south of the border and shake up some cocktails Mexico would be proud of

The Blanco Y Negro cocktail calls for Patrón XO Café, which is tequila-based coffee liqueur that was introduced around 2004. Most coffee liqueurs are low proof and sweet. This one is 70 proof and not so sweet, so the addition of the ginger root maple simple syrup is a nice marriage.

Anyone who has driven around Florida has heard about

the Indian River because of the Indian River fruit stands seen everywhere. The fruit grown around the Indian River is so luscious and juicy that the stands offer to ship gift crates. The river is 140 miles long and runs along the Atlantic coast. Pineapples were introduced to Florida in 1860. Sage can be a little peppery, so the sweetness and spiciness of the Indian River

Blanco Y Negro

Ingredients

2 ounces Patrón XO Café
½ ounce ginger root-infused grade B maple simple syrup
Ice
1 ounce fresh cream
White and dark chocolate stick garnish

1. Chill a 4–5-ounce glass.
2. Shake the Patrón XO Café and ginger root-infused maple simple syrup with ice.
3. Strain into the glass.
4. Gently float fresh cream. Add garnish.

Indian River Sage

Ingredients

Ice
2 ounces common sage and Indian River pineapple-infused 100 percent agave blanco tequila
1 ounce Indian River pineapple puree
½ ounce Citrónge
2 fresh common sage leaves

torn in half
2 ounces fresh Persian lime juice
Common sage sprig garnish clapped between palms to release aroma and oils

1. Chill a cocktail glass with ice.
2. Shake ingredients with ice.
3. Strain into the glass. Add garnish.

sage cocktail create a nice balance.

For the Tea-juana, you'll notice that there are two types of oranges listed. This is because thin-skinned Valencia oranges are best for juicing, and the thick-skinned navel oranges are best for making zests. Ginger beer is nonalcoholic, much like root beer that originated in England in the 1700s. It tastes like ginger ale with a kick. You can find it at your local liquor stores or look for online recipes to make your own.

The most common drinks made with ginger beer are the Moscow Mule and the Dark 'N Stormy. The Moscow Mule was the very first vodka drink introduced to the U.S. in the 1940s. The inventor visited thousands of bars nationwide trying to spread the word about Smirnoff vodka. The Dark 'N Stormy was invented in Bermuda.

Tea-juana

Ingredients

Ice
2 ounces loose carrot cake tea-infused 100 percent agave reposado tequila
1 ounce fresh Meyer lemon juice
1 ounce fresh Valencia orange juice
1 ounce date puree

3 ounces ginger beer
Navel orange zest garnish

1. Chill a cocktail glass with ice.
2. Shake the tequila, juices, and puree with ice.
3. Strain into the glass.
4. Add ginger beer. Add garnish.

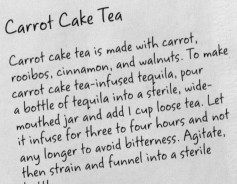

Carrot Cake Tea

Carrot cake tea is made with carrot, rooibos, cinnamon, and walnuts. To make carrot cake tea-infused tequila, pour a bottle of tequila into a sterile, wide-mouthed jar and add I cup loose tea. Let it infuse for three to four hours and not any longer to avoid bitterness. Agitate, then strain and funnel into a sterile bottle.

MODERN WHISKEY COCKTAILS
Pour up some whiskey cocktails using ingredients you've never thought possible

Try the first three modern whiskey cocktails on an autumn or winter day and the fourth in the spring or summer.

To make the walnut-infused Woodford bourbon for Knock on Wood, you'll want to toast 1 cup unshelled walnuts at 400°F for 20 minutes. When finished allow to cool. Pour a bottle of bourbon into a wide-mouthed jar and add walnuts. Let

it sit for 1 week, agitating daily. When finished simply strain and funnel bourbon into a sterilized bottle.

If it's not your season for Clementine (Christmas) oranges, then you can substitute mandarin oranges, and if you can't find those, then use tangerines.

Your curiosity may be piqued when you read about the in-

Knock on Wood

Ingredients

Ice
2 ounces black walnut-infused Woodford Reserve Small Batch Bourbon
1 ounce Christmas orange zest-infused Grade B maple simple syrup
2 dashes Peychaud's bitters
Orange twist garnish

1. Fill a rocks glass with ice.
2. Stir the ingredients with ice.
3. Strain into the glass. Add garnish.

Barrel of Cracker Jacks

Ingredients

Ice
2 ounces real buttered popcorn and roasted peanut-infused Jack Daniel's Single Barrel Whiskey
1 ounce caramel liqueur
2 ounces fresh cream
1 popped caramel popcorn garnish

1. Chill a 4–5-ounce cocktail glass with ice.
2. Shake the infused whiskey and caramel liqueur with ice.
3. Strain into the glass.
4. Top with fresh cream. Add garnish.

fused real buttered popcorn and peanut Jack Daniel's in the Barrel of Cracker Jacks. Yes, modern bartenders have begun to infuse our favorite fats with spirits. To make the infusion, there are three steps but well worth it. First roast ½ cup peanuts and infuse like the walnuts in the Knock on Wood. Strain, then place 2 cups popcorn wrapped in cheesecloth in the Jack Daniel's for 24 hours. Remove the popcorn, then add 1 stick of softened (real) butter and let sit for 4 hours. Place in the freezer so that the fat will rise to the top. Scoop off the fat, and it's ready. When you add caramel liqueur to the recipe,

it will taste like a grownup Cracker Jack drink. The surprise inside is up to you.

Kretek is a word that means "clove cigarettes." Clove comes from the infused Grand Marnier, and the smoke comes from the Islay region Scotch (the smokiest of Scotches). To flame orange oil, funnel essential orange oil to mister, then spray at a flame. It will caramelize over the cocktail.

Kretek

Ingredients

Ice
2 ounces Islay region Scotch whisky
1 ounce clove-infused Grand Marnier
½ ounce fresh Meyer lemon juice
½ ounce fresh Valencia orange juice
Dash of Fee's Whiskey Barrel Aged Bitters
Spray of flamed essential orange oil

1. Chill a 4–5-ounce cocktail glass with ice. Shake all ingredients with ice; strain into glass.
3. Hold a flame over drink, then spray mist of essential orange oil at the flame.

Sweet Rye Reverie

Ingredients

Ice
3 fresh sweet basil leaves (one for garnish)
1 ounce fresh Persian lime juice
2 ounces Sazerac rye whiskey
¼ ounce Carpano Antica
1 ounce pear puree

1. Chill a 5–7-ounce cocktail glass with ice.
2. Muddle two sweet basil leaves and Persian lime juice in a mixing glass.
3. Add ice, rye, Carpano Antica, and puree.
4, Add garnish, then shake with ice and double-strain into the glass.

MODERN BRANDY COCKTAILS

Mix brandy and fruits to craft cocktails that taste like nectar of the gods

Eden is the first place mentioned in any version of the Bible, with apples being the first fruit mentioned in the first chapter of those Bibles. And as you learned in Chapter 4, Laird's Applejack was the first commercial distillery in the U.S., and to continue with this string of firsts there is documented proof that the first president of the United States, George Wash-

ington, wrote to the Laird family requesting the recipe for applejack. Velvet falernum is a paradise-like sweetener that originated in 1890 but was not introduced to America until 2003. With all that information, the Eden cocktail should taste like heaven.

The Pisco Sour has been a popular South American brandy

Ambrosia Navan

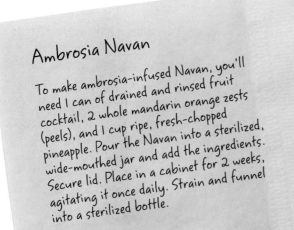

To make ambrosia-infused Navan, you'll need 1 can of drained and rinsed fruit cocktail, 2 whole mandarin orange zests (peels), and 1 cup ripe, fresh-chopped pineapple. Pour the Navan into a sterilized, wide-mouthed jar and add the ingredients. Secure lid. Place in a cabinet for 2 weeks, agitating it once daily. Strain and funnel into a sterilized bottle.

Eden

Ingredients

Organic raw sugar fresh ground cinnamon rim garnish
Ice
2 ounces Laird's Applejack
1 ounce velvet falernum
1 ounce fresh Meyer lemon juice

1. Rim a 4–5-ounce chilled cocktail glass rimmed with cinnamon and raw sugar.
2. Shake the ingredients with ice.
3. Strain into the glass.

cocktail since the late 1800s. The twisted one here uses key lime juice and gomme (pronounced gum). You can purchase gomme syrup through online sources or make your own with sugar, water, and gum powder (gum arabic). Simply mix 1 ounce gum powder with 2 ounces of water. Let sit for 3 hours. Bring 2 cups sugar and 1 cup water to a boil, then add gum powder and bring to a boil again. Remove from heat and skim off the scum that rises to the top with a large spoon. After it is cooled, strain into a sterile bottle. Makes a silky sweetener for your cocktails.

MAKE IT EASY

Make marshmallow orange blossom honey foam by mixing 2 ounces orange blossom honey, 2 ounces marshmallow crème, 1 ounce fresh lemon juice, 3 organic egg whites, and 2 cups filtered water in a bowl. Then transfer to a whipped cream charger. Charge the canister with a nitrous oxide cartridge and place in the fridge for at least 1 hour before using.

Key Lime Pisco Sour

Ingredients

Ice
2 ounces pisco
1 ounce fresh key lime juice
½ ounce gomme
½ organic egg white
1 dash Angostura bitters

1. Chill a 7–9-ounce glass of choice.
2. Shake the ingredients hard with ice.
3. Strain into the glass.
4. Dash bitters on top.

Ambrosia

Ingredients

2 ounces ambrosia-infused Navan
½ ounce DiSaronno Amaretto
3 ounces dry Champagne
Marshmallow orange blossom honey foam garnish
Toasted coconut sprinkle garnish (optional)

1. Shake the infused Navan and amaretto with ice.
2. Strain into the glass.
3. Add Champagne.
4. Add foam.
5. Add coconut garnish (optional)

SIMPLE SYRUP
Learn how simple it is to make one of the key cocktail ingredients

Simple syrup is simply sugar and water mixed together to make a liquid sugar. Sugar in syrup form is the ideal way to add sweetness to a cocktail. Granulated sugar doesn't dissolve as well.

For the simple syrup recipe, a ratio of 1:1 works fine, but some people prefer it a little thicker and will use twice as much sugar as is called for in this recipe. You'll discover your preference after you begin to experiment. For the water, try to use the highest quality available, and for sugar you have choices of raw, organic, brown, and more.

To make infused simple syrup, you simply add clean herbs, fruits, veggies, spices, and so forth to the water. Bring it to a boil, add the sugar, and stir until the sugar is dissolved. Remove from the heat, cover, and allow it to cool and steep. After about 30 minutes you can strain and funnel into a jar or bottle. Simple syrup will keep in the fridge for a month.

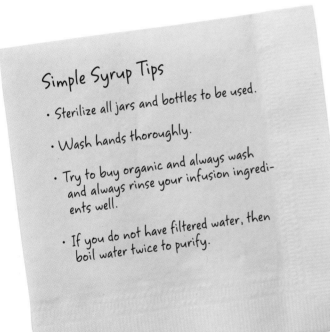

Simple Syrup Tips

- Sterilize all jars and bottles to be used.

- Wash hands thoroughly.

- Try to buy organic and always wash and always rinse your infusion ingredients well.

- If you do not have filtered water, then boil water twice to purify.

Simple Syrup

Ingredients

2 cups water
2 cups sugar

1. Bring the water to a boil.
2. Pour in the sugar. Stir until dissolved.
3. Remove from heat and allow cooling.
4. Funnel into a jar or bottle.

For a no-heat sugar-free simple syrup, use filtered room-temperature water and shake it hard with Splenda in a jar or bottle. You'll notice that the Splenda dissolves very quickly. Simply refrigerate.

· · · · · · · · · · · · · · · GREEN ● LIGHT · · · · · · · · · · · · ·

Simple syrup infusions are limited only to anything that grows in the world that is not toxic. Popular infusions include vanilla, mint, ginger, citrus (use the zested rind), rose petals, lavender, and tea bags. Others to try are roasted coffee beans, peppercorns, and pumpkin. And don't forget that you can combine flavors such as vanilla ginger or cacao bean and chili.

Tri-citrus Infused Simple Syrup

Ingredients

2 cups water
Zest from 1 lime, 1 lemon, and 1 orange
2 cups sugar

1. Bring the water and the citrus zest to a boil.
2. Pour in the sugar. Stir until dissolved.
3. Remove from heat and allow to cool and steep for 30 minutes.
4. Strain and funnel into a jar or bottle.

No-heat Simple Syrup

Ingredients

2 cups sugar
2 cups lukewarm water

1. Funnel the sugar and water into a bottle.
2. Seal cap and shake hard for 10 seconds.
3. Let sit for 1 minute, then shake hard again until sugar is dissolved. Cloudiness will clear.

TECHNIQUES & RECIPES

HONEY & MAPLE SYRUP

Learn more about the birds and the bees and the flowers and the trees

Honey and maple syrup are other sweeteners that can be used to make simple syrup or infused simple syrup to add sweetness to cocktails. As you know, bees make honey from the nectar of flowers. Honey is made all over the world. The most popular honey is from clover, but others that are easily found include alfalfa, buckwheat, wildflower, orange blos-

som, eucalyptus, and blackberry. It all just depends on where the bees buzz. Flavors that mix well with honey are citrus, mint, ginger, hot peppers, vanilla, cinnamon, clove, thyme, rose, lavender, and almond. Alcohols that mix well with honey are vodka, rum, tequila, whiskey, and Champagne.

Maple syrup is made from the sap of maple trees. Vermont

Simple Honey Syrup

Ingredients

2 cups water
2 cups sugar

1. Bring the water to a boil.
2. Pour in the honey. Stir until dissolved.
3. Remove from heat and allow cooling.
4. Funnel into a jar or bottle.

Jalapeño-infused Honey Syrup

Ingredients

2 cups water
1 cup fresh sliced jalapeño peppers
2 cups honey

1. Bring the water and jalapeño peppers to a boil.
2. Pour in the honey. Stir until dissolved.
3. Remove from heat and allow to cool and steep for 30 minutes.
4. Strain and funnel into a jar or bottle.

is the largest producer of maple syrup, but it can be made with sap from any maple tree that grows in a cold climate anywhere. It's divided into two grades: A and B. A grades are lighter and are made from the early maple season, and B grades are darker and from the late season. Flavors that mix well with the flavor of maple syrup include apple, apricot, cranberry, allspice, ginger, cardamom, vanilla, whiskey, mint, and lavender. Alcohols that mix well with maple syrup are whiskey, applejack, and rum.

MAKE IT EASY

Whenever you use dried herbs or spices for infusions, remember to use only half the amount you would use if the herbs or spices were fresh. Growing your own is an option as well. Herbs are probably the simplest plants to learn to grow. And many starter plants can be obtained in local grocery stores in the produce section.

Ginger-infused Maple Syrup

Ingredients

2 cups water
1 cup fresh sliced ginger
2 cups grade B maple syrup

1. Bring the water and ginger to a boil.
2. Pour in the syrup. Stir until dissolved.
3. Remove from heat and allow to cool and steep for 30 minutes.
4. Strain and funnel into a jar or bottle.

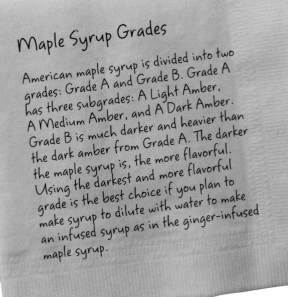

Maple Syrup Grades

American maple syrup is divided into two grades: Grade A and Grade B. Grade A has three subgrades: A Light Amber, A Medium Amber, and A Dark Amber. Grade B is much darker and heavier than the dark amber from Grade A. The darker the maple syrup is, the more flavorful. Using the darkest and more flavorful grade is the best choice if you plan to make syrup to dilute with water to make an infused syrup as in the ginger-infused maple syrup.

INFUSED SPIRITS
Make your own flavored spirits for yourself or for a great gift

If you believe that good things take time, then infusing spirits is right up your alley. To infuse spirits, all you need are alcohol, your chosen infusion ingredients, a wide-mouthed jar, and time. Simply pour the spirit into a sterilized wide-mouthed jar, add the washed and rinsed edible infusion of choice, and seal the top. Set the jar in a cabinet and every day turn it upside down once and back, then set it back in the cabinet. After a few days, you can open the jar and taste-test it.

Some ingredients require a longer infusion but nothing longer than two weeks. Stronger flavors that take only three to four days include vanilla, basil, mint, garlic, dill, oregano, rosemary, citrus rinds, lavender, and thyme. Edibles that take up to a week include pitted cherries, figs, dates, cucumber, apples, raspberries, rose petals, watermelon, peaches, lychees, strawberries, blueberries, blackberries, mangos, and papaya. Fibrous edibles like peppers, lemongrass, ginger, pineapple,

Infused Vodka and Rum

Ingredients

1 750-milliliter bottle premium vodka or rum
3 vanilla beans cut and scraped

1. Pour the vodka or rum into a sterile, wide-mouthed jar.
2. Add vanilla pods. Seal jar.
3. Set in a dark cool place and agitate once daily for four days.
4. Strain and funnel into a sterile jar or bottle.

Cucumber-infused Gin

Ingredients

1 750-milliliter bottle premium gin
2 cups peeled and chopped cucumber

1. Pour gin into a sterile, wide-mouthed jar.
2. Add cucumber. Seal jar.
3. Set in a dark cool place and agitate once daily for one week.
4. Strain and funnel into a sterile jar or bottle.

cinnamon sticks, whole cloves, beans, and chilies take up to two weeks. If you combine flavors, then you may not be able to put them in at the same time.

Some creative infusions use bacon and buttered popcorn. To make infused buttered popcorn rum, air pop 2 cups popcorn, then wrap and tie it in some cheesecloth. Infuse with one 750-milliliter bottle of rum for 24 hours. Remove the popcorn, then add 1 stick of softened (real) butter and let sit for 4 hours. Place in the freezer so the fat will rise to the top. Scoop off the fat, and it's ready. To make bacon-infused bour-bon, simply fry some bacon and pour 2 ounces of the fat and a 750-milliliter bottle of bourbon into a jar. Allow infusing for 4 hours, then follow the freezer procedure.

Coffee and Cacao Bean-infused Tequila

Ingredients

1 750-milliliter bottle premium tequila
½ cup roasted coffee beans
½ cup cacao beans (nips)

1. Pour tequila into a sterile, wide-mouthed jar or jars.
2. Add coffee beans. Seal jar.
3. Set in a dark cool place and agitate once daily for two weeks.
4. Strain and funnel into a sterile jar or bottle.

Cherry-infused Whiskey

Ingredients

1 750-milliliter bottle premium whiskey
2 cups pitted cherries (not maraschinos)

1. Pour whiskey into a sterile, wide-mouthed jar.
2. Add cherries. Seal jar.
3. Set in a dark cool place and agitate once daily for one week.
4. Strain and funnel into a sterile jar or bottle.

INFUSED WATER
Learn century-old ways of aromatizing and flavoring water

Infused water in cocktails adds flavor when you don't want to add the flavor through a sweet infusion or spirit infusion. One popular way by which infused waters are used is misting. Simply funnel the flavored and scented water into a mister, then mist on top of a cocktail. When mixed with a sparkling water or wine, infused waters provide a light, aromatic quality with just a subtle hint of flavor that is perfect for light refreshment.

One of the most important considerations when making infused waters is the quality of the water. Never use water taken straight out of your faucet and then into the pot. You may have a filter on your faucet, but it's best to boil that water at least once for extra purification. Or you can buy distilled or deionized water by the gallon at the grocery store.

The most popular water flavors are infused with nontoxic flower petals. Rose, lavender, hibiscus, and lilac are the most

Water Preservation

Adding 1 ounce of vodka to your infused water and keeping it in the fridge will help preserve it up to a year. Using a dark bottle prolongs life, too, because it reduces the amount of ultraviolet rays that enters the bottle through the glass. Beer, wine, and spirit bottles are darkened for this reason.

Rosewater

Ingredients

3 cups purified water
2 cups clean rose petals
1 ounce vodka

1. Pour purified water and rose petals into a pot.
2. Bring to a boil, then simmer for 30 minutes with a lid on the pot.
3. Allow to cool.
4. Strain and funnel into a sterile jar or bottle. Add vodka.

common. For extra refreshment, you can even spray yourself or your sheets with the water!

The preferred way to make waters requires a large pot with a lid, a 2-cup Pyrex measuring cup, a brick, and some ice. Place a clean brick in the bottom of the pot, then set the Pyrex cup on top of the brick. Fill the pot with your chosen ingredients to the top of the brick, then add distilled water up to the level of the brick. Place the lid on upside down, then bring the water to a boil. Fill the inverted upside-down lid with ice, then lower the temperature to simmer. As the steam rises, the cold lid will cause it to condense and drip into the Pyrex cup. Every 15 minutes empty the cup. This is basic distillation.

These infused waters add flavor without the sweet infusion process.

Cinnamon Apple Water

Ingredients

3 cups purified water
1 cup chopped apples
3 broken cinnamon sticks
1 ounce vodka

1. Pour purified water and apples and cinnamon into a pot.
2. Bring to a boil, then simmer for 30 minutes with a lid on the pot.
3. Allow to cool.
4. Strain and funnel into a sterile jar or bottle. Add vodka.

Turkish Delight Water

Ingredients

3 cups purified water
1 cup clean rose petals
½ cup fresh mint leaves
½ cup natural unshelled pistachio nuts
1 broken cinnamon stick
1 ounce vodka

1. Pour all the ingredients except the vodka into a pot.
2. Bring to a boil, then simmer for 30 minutes with a lid on the pot.
3. Allow to cool.
4. Strain and funnel into a sterile jar or bottle. Add vodka.

PUREES

Use your food processor and mash up full-bodied flavors for your cocktail

Purees add bursting, concentrated flavor to a cocktail. The most common purees on the market are in the baby food aisle at your local grocer. Of course, nothing compares with making your own purees, but scan the baby food for ideas anyway!

Making purees is pretty simple. Basically, you peel and chop your chosen carbohydrate, then heat it and mash it up. Heating options include baking, boiling, and steaming. The preferred method is steaming because it keeps a lot of the flavor and vitamins intact. Baking is fine, but it takes a long time and uses a lot of energy. After your puree is heated, simply use a food processor to mash it up. At this point, you can mix in

Peach Puree

Ingredients

1 pound peaches (about 4) skinned, pitted, and chopped
1 ounce simple syrup if desired

1. Steam peaches until soft.
2. Place in the food processor for 1 minute.
3. Taste, then add simple syrup if desired.
4. Spoon into sterile jars or containers. Refrigerate.
Yields 1 cup

Tropical Puree

Ingredients

1 mango peeled, pitted, and chopped
1 cup chopped fresh pineapple
1 ripe banana
1 ounce simple syrup or falernum if desired

1. Steam mango and pineapple until soft.
2. Place in the food processor with the banana for 1 minute.
3. Taste, then add simple syrup or falernum if desired.
4. Spoon into sterile jars or containers. Refrigerate.
Yields 1 cup

more ingredients or other purées with it if desired. Then the mash gets spooned straight into small sterile jars. You can also use simple disposable plasticware. Some people prefer to push the puree through a sieve for extra straining first.

Keep the puree in the fridge for preservation. You can also freeze the puree in ice trays. When it's frozen, pop out the puree cubes and store in a freezer bag for future use. You can use them in the blender for a frozen drink or allow them to thaw.

ZOOM

The tropical puree can contain any of your favorite tropical fruits, such as papaya, mandarin oranges, lychees, kiwi, and tangerines. Cornucopia puree can contain any autumn, winter, and harvest edibles such as pears, squash, ground nuts, cranberries, persimmons, oranges, and ground allspice. You could even make a spa puree with cucumber, mint, and lemons.

Cornucopia Puree

Ingredients

1 cup skinned, chopped, and seeded red apple
1 cup chopped pumpkin meat
1 teaspoon ground cinnamon
1 ounce simple syrup or honey syrup if desired

1. Steam apple and pumpkin until soft.
2. Place in the food processor with the cinnamon for 1 minute.
3. Taste, then add simple syrup or honey syrup if desired.
4. Spoon into sterile jars or containers. Refrigerate.
Yields 1 cup

Easy Skinning

You can skin fruit with a knife, but with some fruit it's easier to boil it first. Bring a large pot of water to a boil, then drop in the fruit. Boil for 5–10 minutes, then remove from the pot and set on a towel to cool. When it is cool, you can easily remove the skins of the fruit.

TECHNIQUES & RECIPES

221

HOMEMADE CLASSIC DRINK MIXES
Try your hand at making essential bar mixers in your own kitchen

Two of the most confusing mixers to the layperson are margarita mix and sweet-and-sour mix. That's no surprise because any mixer aisle at liquor stores offers a wide assortment . . . full of fake colorings and words you can't pronounce to ensure shelf life, if I may add.

The first thing you should know is that margarita mix has a lime base and sour mix has a lemon base. You wouldn't make a whiskey sour with margarita mix, and you shouldn't make a margarita with sour mix. The next thing to know is that each mix should contain only three ingredients: water, sugar, and citrus juice. That's it. Now stop for a minute and flip back through some recipes in this book, and you'll see that many of them call for 1 ounce lemon juice and 1 ounce simple syrup. That's sour mix (a little bit of sweet and a little bit of sour)! Look at the margaritas in the margarita chapter, and you'll see 1 ounce lime juice and I ounce simple syrup. That's margarita

Margarita Mix

Ingredients

2 cups fresh lime juice
2 cups simple syrup

1. Mix the juice and simple syrup together.
2. Pour into a sterile bottle. Refrigerate.

Sweet-and-sour Mix

Ingredients

2 cups fresh lemon juice
2 cups simple syrup

1. Mix the juice and simple syrup together.
2. Pour into a sterile bottle. Refrigerate.

mix! And in some recipes you'll see that simple syrup can be replaced by other sweeteners such as grenadine, honey, and agave syrup. Some people like to make an all-purpose sour mix that uses half lemon and half lime juice, and that's fine for lots of tropical drinks, but it limits you with other drinks.

When mixing the simple syrup and juice together, your goal is to reach a balance of sweet and sour. Feel free to adjust the sweetness or sour, depending on your taste preferences. Also, don't forget that you can make a sugar-free mix by using Splenda simple syrup.

Just so you know, grenadine was originally made from pomegranates. Through time, companies began using cheaper ingredients such as cherry syrups to substitute.

Grenadine

Ingredients

2 cups pomegranate juice
1 cup granulated sugar
1 ounce vodka

1. Heat the pomegranate juice to a simmer.
2. Stir in the sugar until dissolved.
3. Funnel into a sterile bottle. Add vodka. Refrigerate.

No-heat Grenadine

You can also make no-heat grenadine by placing 1 cup of pomegranate juice and 1 cup of granulated sugar in a jar. Seal tightly, then shake hard until the sugar is dissolved. You may need to shake again. You can also keep adding sugar and juice until you make the amount you need.

223

RESOURCES
Cream of the Crop

While this is not a complete list of resources, it is enough to help point you in the correct direction. Links and resources from these Web sites will guide you further. One caveat: Know that there are many people in the world that claim to be a "professional" and that the word professional is thrown around to mean many things to many people. Rest assured, however, that the following listed can be used to guide you like the Northern star would.

RESOURCES

Bar & Drink Supplies

Barproducts.com
www.barproducts.com
• Every bar tool seen in this book came from barproducts.com. It has been selling bar supplies since 1995 and is the official supply store for *Nightclub and Bar* magazine.

Fee Brothers
www.feebrothers.com
• Fee Brothers is a four-generation-old (since 1863) manufacturer of top-quality cocktail mixes, bitters, and flavoring syrups. Look here first when searching for an unusual ingredient in this book like assorted bitters, falernum, gomme, and orgeat.

LeNell's Ltd.
www.lenells.com
• This wine and spirit boutique specializes in hard-to-find spirits, so if you see an ingredient in this book that you cannot find at your local liquor store, try LeNell's.

Spirit Foodservice, Inc.
www.spiritfoodservice.com
• Spirit Foodservice, Inc. makes custom and specialty drink stirrers, specialty straws, novelty cocktail picks, and other goodies for your drinks. It has been around since 1934.

Top Cocktail Connoisseurs, Modern Mixologists, & Liquid Chefs

Angus Winchester
www.barmetrix.com
• Angus is a veteran bartender of twenty years. He is an ambassador for the modern professional bartender, traveling the world hosting training sessions and tastings. Angus also owns and maintains www.alconomics.com and www.therumclub.com.

Anistatia Miller and Jared Brown
martiniplace.com
www.euvs.org
www.mixellany.com
• Anistatia Miller and Jared Brown are credited with establishing the first bar and cocktail Web site (martiniplace.com) on the Internet in 1995. Today they are the directors/curators of Exposition Universelle des Vins et Spiritueux on Ile de Bendor, France. They are also publishers of *Mixologist: The Journal of the American Cocktail*, the scholarly journal on cocktails and spirits of the Museum of the American Cocktail, of which they are co-founders.

Ardent Spirits
www.ardentspirits.com
• Gary Regan is a spirit and cocktail expert and author of many books, including *The Joy of Mixology*. He also maintains a worldwide bartender newsletter that keeps up with all the latest drink trends and happenings.

CocktailDB
www.cocktaildb.com
• Ted "Dr. Cocktail" Haigh is a cocktail historian, speaker, consultant, and author of *Vintage Spirits and Forgotten Cocktails*. He is also the curator for the Museum of the American Cocktail and co-founder of cocktaildb.com. He lives in Los Angeles.

Darcy O'Neil
www.theartofdrink.com
• Darcy O'Neil is a bartender and chemist in London, Ontario. He publishes *The Art of Drink* and writes cocktail-related articles for many publications.

DrinkBoy
www.drinkboy.com
• Seattle-based Robert Hess owns DrinkBoy.com. The site is dedicated to providing clear and concise information about the art of the cocktail.

Jamie Boudreau
www.spiritsandcocktails.com
• Jamie's thirst for cocktail minutia is infamous, and if conversation turns to a subject that he is unsure of, you can be assured that he will research it as soon as possible. He has a love for the classics but at the same time is always

looking for new, exciting ingredients with which to try out new recipes. He is known for his molecular mixology.

Jeff Berry
www.beachbumberry.com
- Jeff "Beachbum" Berry is the author of *Beachbum Berry's Grog Log,* which the *New York Times* hailed as the world's first serious tiki cocktail book. Jeff is the world authority on all tiki cocktails, and his creations have been featured in many publications and served in famous bars around the world. Jeff serves on the advisory board of the Museum of the American Cocktail.

Jeffery Morgenthaler
www.jeffreymorgenthaler.com
- Jeffrey Morgenthaler is a master mixologist who writes about bartending and mixology from Eugene, Oregon.

King Cocktail
www.kingcocktail.com
- Dale "King Cocktail" Degroff is credited with pioneering the revival of the classic cocktail. He's the world's foremost mixologist and is the president and founder of the Museum of the American Cocktail and the author of *The Craft of the Cocktail.*

The Modern Mixologist
www.themodernmixologist.com
- Las Vegas-based Tony Abou-Ganim is a leader in the beverage industry who can be seen on *Iron Chef* and demonstrates the art of cocktail preparation on the

Fine Living Network program *Raising the Bar.* He also runs his own beverage consulting firm.

Natalie Bovis-Nelsen
www.theliquidmuse.com
- Los Angeles-based author, cocktail blogger, mixologist, spirits columnist, and online cocktail show host Natalie Bovis-Nelsen has a passion for cocktail culture that defines her career. As editor and blogger of TheLiquidMuse.com, Natalie keeps a close eye on drink trends, the people who set them, and bars around the world where connoisseurs can share a quality tipple.

Paul Clarke
www.cocktailchronicles.com
- The Cocktail Chronicles Web site is owned by Paul Clarke, a Seattle-based cocktail enthusiast. His site is an ongoing exploration of fine spirits, creative cocktails, and classic mixology.

Simon Difford
www.diffordsguide.com
- Simon Difford is best known for his yearly color recipe book, *Difford's Guide to Cocktails.* Simon constantly travels the world in search of the best bars and their best cocktails.

Stanislav Vadrna
www.stanislavvadrna.com
- Stan is from Bratislava, Slovakia. He first made cocktail history when he won a world cocktail menu contest for the bar he worked at called "Paparazzi." Since

then he has founded Stanislav Vadrna's School of Bartending and Mixology and a joint project with the Redmonkeygroup.

Stephen Beaumont
www.worldofbeer.com
- Stephen Beaumont has been documenting the world of beer, spirits, food, and travel for almost twenty years. He writes for many related blogs, including www.thatsthespirit.com and www.onthehouse.typepad.com.

Other leaders in the industry who do not have a Web site are Francesco Lafranconi, David Wondrich, Audrey Saunders, Charlotte Voisey, Bridget Albert, Phil Greene, and Chris and Laura McMillian.

EVENTS AND CONFERENCES

February/March

Nightclub & Bar Convention and Trade Show

www.nightclub.com

Nightclub & Bar hosts many conventions throughout the year, but the world's largest is in Las Vegas.

March/April

Cocktail Film Fest

www.talesofthecocktail.com

The Cocktail Film Fest takes place in New Orleans and is put on by Tales of the Cocktail. Films with cocktails in them are shown, and movie buffs and libation lovers are served food and drink seen in the films. There is lots of themed fun, and it's hosted by Cheryl Charming.

May

San Francisco Cocktail Week

www.sfcocktailweek.com

This week honors San Francisco's vibrant cocktail culture. Local bartenders access local farmers, local distilleries, and local wineries and devour cocktail lore, pair with chefs, and teach each other to create delicious cocktails. They strive to remember the past in order to balance the new. They also celebrate both the classic cocktail concoction and the avant-garde potation.

World Cocktail Week

www.museumoftheamericancocktail.org/WCD

World Cocktail Week was established to celebrate the rich history of the cocktail and recognize the craftsmanship and skill of the bartenders who have been mixing them for over two hundred years. Events are organized worldwide so that you can celebrate at the event closest to you.

June

The Bar Show

www.newyorkbarshow.com

The Bar Show is the only trade show specifically for professionals representing the bar, nightclub, restaurant, and liquor store industry. It is held in at the Jacob K. Javits Convention Center in New York City.

Hukilau

www.thehukilau.com

Hukilau is four days of tiki tunes, treasures, live entertainment, special guests, and, of course, tiki cocktails. Most events take place at the Yankee Clipper Hotel and at the Mai-Kai in Fort Lauderdale, Florida.

July

Tales of the Cocktail

www.talesofthecocktail.com

Tales of the Cocktail is the culinary and cocktail festival that features award-winning mixologists, authors, bartenders, chefs, and designers in the New Orleans French Quarter at five days of cocktail events such as dinner pairings, cocktail demos, tastings, seminars, mixing competitions, design expos, and book signings. Visitors worldwide attend this event.

RESOURCES

LEARNING TO BARTEND

The Best Bartender Training

BarSmarts
www.barsmarts.com

• BarSmarts Advanced is the only comprehensive spirits, mixology, and service education and certification program available today. Candidates are given a BarSmarts invitation with a registration code and then their BarSmarts kit in the mail. The kit contains a BarSmarts DVD, workbook, and a set of professional bar tools (hand selected by Dale DeGroff). Candidates study the materials at their own pace. After each module, candidates go back online to take a quiz (total of four), which assists them in getting ready for the final exam at BarSmarts Live.

• When all four modules of the DVD, workbook, and quizzes are complete, the program culminates with BarSmarts Live, a dynamic, full day of seminars, discussions, hands-on mixology, testing, and certification.

Beverage Alcohol Resource (BAR)
www.beveragealcoholresource.com

• Beverage Alcohol Resource in New York City was the first culinary mixology course. Its graduates are able to mix a balanced sidecar, distinguish a Speyside malt from a Lowland malt, explain in detail the difference between bourbon whiskey and Irish whiskey, recognize when a tequila is overpriced, identify a potato vodka by its nose alone, explain the origin of the manhattan cocktail and why the bitters are an integral part of the drink, draw up a cocktail list that matches the elegance of the establishment it's created for, and, in short, do everything that one expects from an educated professional to educate, guide, and propagate the healthy, enlightened, and responsible use of beverage alcohol products.

Gary Regan's Weekend Cocktails in the Country Bartending Classes
www.ardentspirits.com

• Gary's bartender classes, called "Cocktails in the Country," are an intensive two-day course in the craft of the cocktailian bartender. They are aimed specifically at professional bar, restaurant, and hotel employees.

Organizations

Museum of the American Cocktail
www.museumoftheamericancocktail.org

• The Museum of the American Cocktail is a nonprofit organization that celebrates a true American cultural icon: the American cocktail. It welcomes a global network of the

most passionate and talented bartenders, collectors, historians, and writers on the subject of drink.

U.S. Bartenders Guild

www.usbg.org

- The purpose of the U.S. Bartenders Guild is to improve customer-bartender relations, increase the prestige of bartenders, and perform public relations for the alcoholic beverage industry.

Best Cocktail Consultants to Learn From

Bar Magic

www.barmagic.com

- Bar Magic, LLC is a Las Vegas-based unique drink design business owned by Tobin Ellis. Tobin provides worldwide services for development, operations, and marketing services for hospitality, foodservice, and nightlife operations.

BarMedia

www.barmedia.com

- Robert Plotkin is BarMedia. His mission is to serve the needs of aspiring professionals and enlighten the social host on the nuances of creative mixology.

Cuff & Buttons

www.cuffandbuttons.com

- Cuff & Buttons is a partnership between three bartenders from New York City's cocktail vanguard. It brings together the talents of Sasha Petraske, Christy Pope, and Chad Solomon.

Liquid Architecture

www.liquid-architecture.com

- Liquid Architecture is a beverage consultancy owned by Kim Haasarud who creates signature liquid cuisine and bar concepts into beverage masterpieces.

Liquid Relations

www.liquidrelations.com

- Ryan Magarian heads Liquid Relations, a beverage development company based in Seattle. He has a unique, cheflike approach to the craft of mixology and develops innovative bar programs.

Liquid Solutions

www.liquidsolutions.org

- Philip Duff heads Liquid Solutions. He is a renowned bar and beverage consultant and award-winning mixologist who travels the world to advise and train major drinks companies, hotels, bars, restaurants, and nightclubs about brands, bartending, and cocktails.

Performance Bartending

FBA (Flair Bartenders Association)

www.barflair.org

- Since 1997 the goal of FBA has been to help teach the art of flair, promote the sport of freestyle or extreme bartending, and support all styles of performance bartending in a safe and fun manner worldwide. If you are looking for a flair bartender in your part of the country for a party, then know that membership is not required to use the Web site forums.

Flair Bar

www.flairbar.com

- *Flair Bar* is a monthly e-zine that keeps you updated with current flair bartending events and trends.

Flairco

www.flairco.com

- Dean Serneels is the inventor of the original flair practice bottle and bar unit that folds up into a suitcase. He also is head of the Flairco Bartending Arts and Sciences Training Program.

BARS AND LOUNGES
Dedicated to the Craft of the Cocktail

California: San Francisco

Absinthe Brasserie and Bar

www.absinthe.com
398 Hayes St.
(415) 551-1590

- Absinthe Brasserie and Bar is one of the most romantic and popular fine-dining establishments in San Francisco, serving classic and creative upscale American-influenced French brasserie as well as an extensive handcrafted cocktail menu.

Bourbon & Branch

www.bourbonandbranch.com
501 Jones St.
Phone number and password are gained only by registering online for a reservation.

- Bourbon & Branch is a throwback to the 1920s and the era of Prohibition when the sale and consumption of alcoholic beverages were outlawed. You'll experience the ambience of that time in an actual speakeasy that operated illegally at its location from 1921 to 1933. There are rules here: Do not use a cell phone, smoke only out back, do not stand at the bar, and be patient for labor-intensive cocktails.

Cantina

www.cantinasf.com
580 Sutter St.
(415) 398-0195

- Cantina is a Latin abode, an art salon, and a culinary cocktail lounge featuring wines and spirits shaken and poured in nouveau ways. Owned by master mixologist Duggan McDonnell.

Elixir

www.elixirsf.com
16th and Guerrero
(415) 552-1633

- The first certified green bar in San Francisco, Elixir has an expansive cocktail menu and a spirits collection that focuses on the vintage, the organic, the local, and the original, all while remaining a friendly corner bar. Owned by H. Joseph Ehrmann.

Forbidden Island Tiki Lounge

www.forbiddenislandalameda.com
1304 Lincoln Ave.
(510) 749-0332

- Forbidden Island Tiki Lounge serves vintage tropical drinks and modern cocktails made perfectly balanced with fresh-squeezed, seasonal juices and premium ingredients.

Tommy's Mexican Restaurant

www.tommystequila.com
5929 Geary Blvd.
(415) 387-4747

- Tequila guru Julio Bermejo works at Tommy's Mexican Restaurant. He is known by everyone in the industry and will remember you. The bar is small and is decorated with nothing but 100 percent agave tequila. Julio has a team of Mexicans who work like oompa-loompas squeezing fresh limes for made-to-order tequila cocktails. It's an experience not to be missed.

Florida: Fort Lauderdale

Mai-Kai

www.maikai.com
3599 N. Federal Highway (U.S. 1)
(954) 563-3272

- The Mai-Kai is the sole survivor of America's grand midcentury tiki supper clubs; its stellar tiki cocktails, food, and decor provide an experience unmatched for anyone.

Florida: South Beach/Miami

The Florida Room

www.delano-hotel.com
Delano Hotel
1685 Collins
(305) 672-2000

- The Florida Room is an intimate speakeasy that evokes a bygone era and serves handcrafted specialty cocktails imbued with a Cuban/Latin feel. The room has a Lucite grand piano that has been played by music legends such as Lenny Kravitz and Jamie Foxx.

Louisiana: New Orleans

Arnaud's French 75 Bar

www.arnauds.com/bar.html
813 Rue Beinville
(504) 523-5433

- The French 75 Bar has been in Arnaud's since 1918. The crafted drink menu is extensive, with drinks ranging from the cocktail for which the bar is named to a dizzying selection of martinis and other cocktails. Look for master mixologist Chris Hanna.

Carousel Bar

www.hotelmonteleone.com
Monteleone Hotel

214 Rue Royale
(504) 523-3341

- The Carousel Bar is immortalized in the writings of Ernest Hemingway and others. The historic bar top and stools take you on a slow, fifteen-minute ride around the bar. Look for master mixologist Marvin Allen for a crafted historic cocktail.

Swizzle Stick Bar

www.swizzlestickbar.com
Loews New Orleans Hotel
300 Poydras St.
(504) 595-3305
- The Swizzle Stick Bar was inspired by the famous Brennans' beloved Aunt Adelaide, who personified the avant-garde cocktail culture of the late 1950s and 1960s, and represents the joie de vivre of all that is New Orleans.

New York: New York City

Death + Company

www.deathandcompany.com
433 East 6th St.
(212) 388-0882
- Death + Company is a restaurant/bar that celebrates the golden age of the cocktail of days gone by and of today. The crafted cocktail menu is extensive. No reservations. First come, first served.

Flatiron Lounge

www.flatironlounge.com
37 W. 19th St.
(212) 727-7741
- Flatiron Lounge is co-owned by bar chef Julie Reiner. She draws much of her inspiration from her native Hawaii by utilizing the freshest fruits and the highest-quality spices and spirits available.

PDT

www.pdtnyc.com
113 St. Mark's Place
(212) 614-0386
- PDT (Please Don't Tell) is a modern, Prohibition-era speakeasy serving crated cocktails. Some on the menu, such as bacon-infused bourbon, are extreme. The entrance is not seen from the street, and there is no sign. The front door is located inside an adjacent store (Crif Dogs hot dogs) and is camouflaged as a phone booth. Once inside the booth, you lift the receiver, hit the call button, and wait for the person on the other side to let you in.

Milk & Honey

www.mlkhny.com/newyork
134 Eldridge St.
- The tiny Milk & Honey bar is a true speakeasy that has a constantly changing phone number and requires a password for admission. There is no visible entrance, and everything is freshly made, from the ice to the bitters. The owner, Sasha Petraske, created the bar in personal retaliation against celebrity-obsessed nightlife. Only nonfamous folk receive the unlisted phone numbers and must call ahead to be buzzed in through the surveillance system-equipped door.

Pegu Club

www.peguclub.com
77 West Houston St., 2nd floor
(212) 473-PEGU
- Pegu Club was opened by cocktail goddess Audrey Saunders and bar chef Julie Reiner. Located in Manhattan's Soho district, it is revered by cocktail enthusiasts as one of the best cocktail lounges in the world. The name pays tribute to a storied, late-nineteenth-century British

officers club in Burma (Myanmar), which has since closed.

Oregon: Portland

Mint/820

www.mintand820.com
816 North Russell
(503) 284-5518
- Mint/820 is owned by Lucy Brennan. Lucy is at the forefront of creating cocktails that incorporate fresh fruit and food into each drink and has been noted as one of the top mixologists in the country by *Food and Wine* and *Bon Appetit* magazines.

Teardrop Lounge

www.teardroplounge.com
1015 NW Everett St.
(503)445-8109
- This lounge offers lovingly made libations with crafted mixers, tinctures, specialty liqueurs in liquid culinary style. Cultivated by master mixologist Daniel Shoemaker.

Washington: Seattle

Zig Zag Café

www.zigzagcafe.net
1501 Western Ave.
(206) 625-1146
- The award-winning Zig Zag Café was born from the desire to provide its patrons with an unprecedented selection of the finest spirits. One bartender, Murray Stenson, is widely revered and universally beloved. Murray has been serving cocktails in Seattle for over thirty years, inspiring scores of cocktail aficionados and fellow bartenders along the way.

THE BEST OF THE REST

Podcasts and Weblogs

The Cocktail Spirit with Robert Hess
www.smallscreennetwork.com

Tiki Bar TV
www.tikibartv.com

iPhone Applications

Cocktails
You can download over a thousand cocktail and mixed drink recipes in your pocket. Impress your friends and discover your next favorite drink among the same classic recipes that inspire today's top bartenders.

Magazines

Imbibe
www.imbibemagazine.com
Imbibe is the magazine of liquid culture. It has a completely new way of looking at drinks—as a distinct culinary category deserving in-depth exploration of history, ingredients, preparation, artistry, and consumption.

Cheers!

www.beveragenet.net

Cheers! is written for owners and food and beverage managers of premium full-service establishments: chain and independent hotels, restaurants, clubs, caterers, and bars serving wine, beer, and spirits. The editorial focus is on product knowledge, merchandise and promotions, industry trends and developments, employee training, and other business aspects.

Santé

www.santemagazine.com

Santé is an award-winning national magazine for restaurant and hospitality professionals.

Sites of Interest

www.misscharming.com
www.cocktails.about.com
www.knackbooks.com

INDEX

235

INDEX